MIDNIGHT MARQUEE
Number 73/74

Editors
Gary J. Svehla
Susan Svehla

Managing Editor
Richard J. Svehla

Copy Editor
Linda J. Walter

Graphic Design Interior
Gary J. Svehla

**Cover Design/
Title Page Design**
Susan Svehla

Contributing Writers
Anthony Ambrogio, Richard Bojarski, Mark Clark, David J. Hogan, James J.J. Janis, Jonathan M. Lampley, Arthur Joseph Lundquist, Jeff Miller, Bryan Senn, Cindy Collins Smith, Brian Smith, Kenny Strong, Gary J. Svehla, Steven Thornton, Robert Tinnell, Nathalie Yafet

Acknowledgments
John Antosiewicz Photo Archives, Eric Caidin, Jerry Ohlinger's Movie Material Store, Photofest/Buddy Weiss, Kenny Strong

Illustrator
Allen J. Koszowski

Publisher
Midnight Marquee Press

Midnight Marquee
Number 73/74
Copyright 2005 © by Gary J. Svehla
  Published twice yearly by Midnight Marquee Press at $17 per year. Printed by Boyd Printing, Albany, NY.
  Return postage must accompany articles and art, if the owner wants them returned. No responsibility is taken for unsolicited material. Editorial views expressed by our contributors are not necessarily those of the publisher. Nothing may be reproduced in any media without written permission of the publisher. Send submissions of articles, letters and art to Gary J. Svehla, 9721 Britinay Lane, Baltimore, MD 21234; web site: http://www.midmar.com; e-mail: mmarquee@aol.com
  Letters of comment addressed to Midnight Marquee or Gary or Susan Svehla will be considered for publication unless the writer requests otherwise. Subscription rates: $10 per single copy or $17 per year (shipped U.S. Media Mail). Subscription copies are mailed in sturdy cardboard mailers and will arrive in excellent condition; support MidMar by becoming a direct-mail subscriber. Foreign orders are $39 (U.S.) for a two issue subscription. This issue is dedicated to Mike Woodin, whose loyalty, dedication and friendship is unwavering.

TABLE OF CONTENTS

3   Marquee Mutterings: Editorial
by Gary J. Svehla

6   The Ferociously Compelling Barbara Steele in *Nightmare Castle*
by David J. Hogan

14   Frank Strayer: Poverty Row's Dark Director
by Kenny Strong

24   Forum/Against 'Em: *The Devil Commands* vs. *The Man Who Changed His Mind*
edited by Anthony Ambrogio

34   *Black Friday*: Universal's Horror Fraud
by Nathalie Yafet

40   Bad Moon Rising: *Ginger Snaps* and *Dog Soldiers*
by Gary J. Svehla

51   *Monster That Challenged the World*... and *Jaws*
by Jeff Miller

57   DVD Reviews
by Gary J. Svehla

92   Book Reviews

94   Grave Diggings [Letters]

Marquee Mutterings

Our excuse for the lateness of the last issue was the birth of our third magazine, *Movie Mystique*, which was now dividing our energies in three separate directions. This latest issue is not as late, simply because we are back to only publishing two magazines, as our experiment with *Movie Mystique* only survived two brief issues. Our goal was to investigate fresh and exciting modern horror cinema, with glossy pages and full color layout on every page. Such a magazine was very expensive to publish, and the sales were simply not enough to cover the printing bills. We cut our losses early. Many of the features intended for *Movie Mystique* will now be carried in *Midnight Marquee*. Our focus will still be on the classic horror cinema of the past, but once in a while a feature on original modern films such as *Ginger Snaps* and *Dog Soldier* (thanks to friend Leo Dymowski for turning me on to these wonderful movies) would seem to be in order.

For everyone thinking of updating to digital HD plasma or LCD televisions with surround sound systems, now is the time to seriously consider going with a video projector and a screen. Even if you do not have the room for a truly dedicated home theater, a den or family room or even an attic, even with ambient light, can become a true home theater at a cost that will rival going plasma or big screen. For instance, an entire new generation of home theater projectors, DLP with HD2+ chips, that formerly sold for upwards of $10,000 or more, are now being released at street prices of $3,000 to $4,000. And these projectors will fill a seven, eight or even nine-foot 16:9 screen without any problem. This means actual projected movies on a bright screen duplicating the movie theater experience. It cannot be beat! Add a home theater receiver, DVD player, digital cable or satellite TV receiver and speaker system and the entire thing can be done for $10,000 or less. Sue and I simply never go to the mall cineplex anymore when we have the comfort of the ultimate big screen experience here at home. I just became guru to friend "Ace" Wittig, who created a home theater in his townhouse basement for this very budget, and his theater rocks! Folks, why settle for anything less!!!!

Unfortunately, friend, *Midnight Marquee* contributor and FANEX participant John E. Parnum lost his battle to throat cancer last July at the age of 68. Unlike most of the current magazine staffers, Parnum was one generation older, a fan who actually saw *House of Frankenstein* upon its original theatrical release and met Boris Karloff backstage during one of his theater performances. Parnum, whose infectious smile erupted whenever he was chatting with a group of horror movie fans (John's inner "little boy" always thrived), was always haunting convention dealers rooms, armed with his trusty deteriorating briefcase that had seen better days, looking for those pressbooks and lobby cards he needed to complete his collection. During the late 1960s when jeans were the thing, Parnum proved his independence by wearing Bermuda shirts to shows when he was the only person wearing shorts. His energetic and passionate tributes to guests at FANEX were often punctuated with mispronunciations of guest names (Michael Pate—rhymes with "date"—became Michael "Pat-taaaa"; Eleana Verdugo, where "Ah-LANE-na" became "EL-la-na"), but such was John's charm. It even got to the point that John would rehearse his FANEX speeches with Sue to make sure he got the names right. One of his proudest FANEX moments was being part of the team who gave Forry Ackerman a lifetime achievement award.

During his final decade John coped with diabetes, open heart bypass surgery, a brutal mugging and beating in a Philadelphia mall parking garage (afterwards he proudly displayed photos showing the results of such a beating, taken a day or so following his pummeling) and throat cancer caused by having his inflamed tonsils treated with doses of radiation during his youth. But even when things were going wrong, John proudly detailed his progress with his

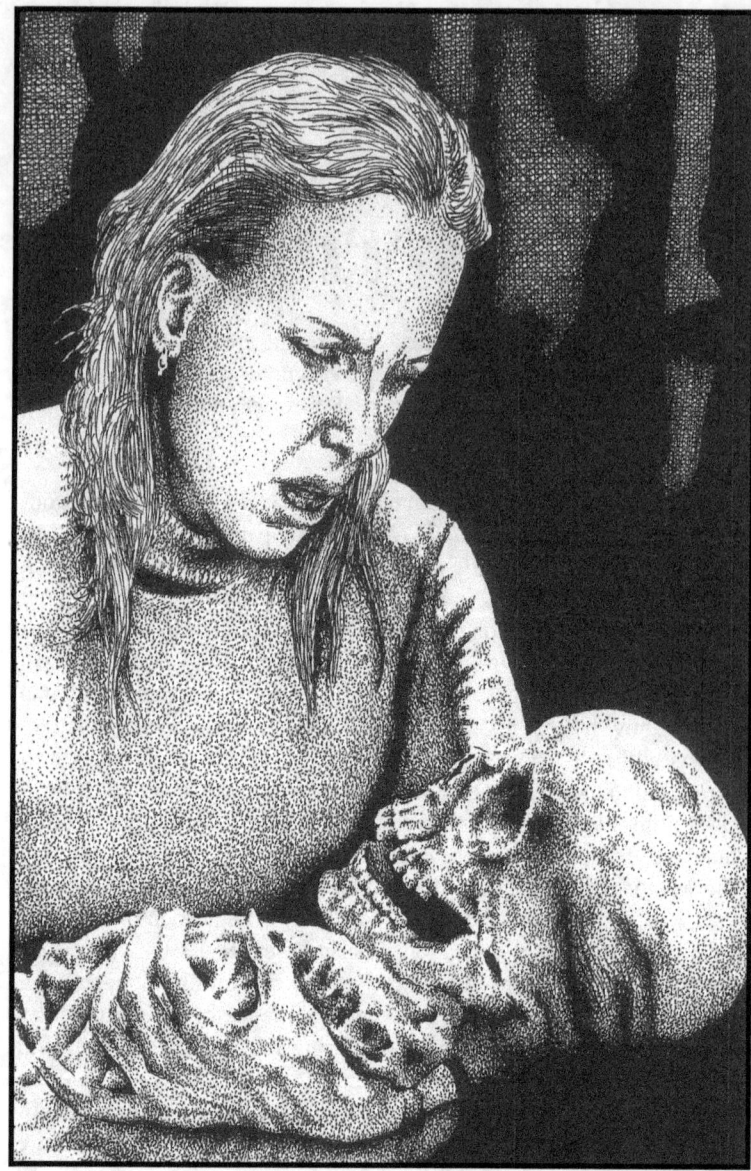

Frankenstein and *Frankenstein Meets the Wolf Man*—were on display as his life was celebrated with poignant and humorous anecdotes. We should all be so lucky to live such a rich life.

Since last issue, the Classic Horror Film Forums moved from their AOL-exclusive message boards where only AOL subscribers could partake in the fun. AOL monitoring started to get ridiculous and such censorship became the bane of both the board administrators and posters. So Kerry Gammill's Monster Kid Forums became the home of the new Classic Horror Film Forums, with original founder David Colton (Taraco) coming along for the ride. Magically, with few exceptions, the new forums are filled with the spirit of camaraderie and enthusiasm with nary a flame war in sight. These forums are on the popular EZ Boards where anybody can access, read and post. Now the regular crew from AOL is being joined almost weekly by new names such as Dick Klemensen and Mark Frank and others. For classic horror movie lovers, such forums are informative and fun, and while it is sometimes difficult to crack the

health and his collection via email, and was on cloud nine when he finally was able to secure the Realart title lobby card from *Frankenstein*, the last elusive piece in his Frankenstein collection, mere months before his death. His monster movie collection was housed in the basement of his Wayne, PA home where he hosted a home theater with projector, the original one that influenced me to add a home theater to our home. John, who was always morbidly curious, made an audiotape about a week before his demise literally "speaking from beyond the grave" at his memorial service to all the assembled friends and family. In a weakened yet playful voice, John read a poem or two and reflected upon his own morality. Several of his movie posters—inserts from *Ghost of*

boys' club closeness of the core group, new posters are always welcome.

Check them out at http://pub20.ezboard.com/bmonsterkidclassichorrorforum and join the over 500 registered members.

Lastly, we are elated that many new writers are beginning to submit work to all our magazines. We survived for over 40 years because of our willingness to give unpublished authors a shot. So keep letters and articles coming. Just check out our Writers' Style Sheet on our web site before submitting articles. Enough for now. Enjoy the issue!

Gary J. Svehla

MIDNIGHT MARQUEE BACK ISSUES

33 - $6   37 - $10   38 - $6   42 - $10   43 - $10   44 - $40
45 - $20   46 - $10   48 - $20   49 - $20   50 - $6   51 - $20
53 - $6   54 - $6   55 - $6   56 - $6   57 - $6   58 - $6
59 - $6   60 - $6   61 - $6   62 - $6   63 - $6   64 - $6
65/66 - $10   67/68 - $10   69/70 - $10   71/72 - $10   Mad About Movies #3 - $10   Mad About Movies #4 - $10

Midnight Marquee has finally caught up with our subscribers
and will being single issue numbers starting with #75.
Subscribe to *Midnight Marquee* or *Mad About Movies* for $17 a year or $34 two years,
or $30 for one year of *Midnight Marquee* and *Mad About Movies*.

Midnight Marquee Press, 9721 Britinay Lane, Baltimore, MD 21234; 410-665-1198; www.midmar.com

The Ferociously Compelling BARBARA STEELE in NIGHTMARE CASTLE

by David J. Hogan

Some things in life demand our gaze with particular urgency: a dynamited high-rise as it sinks to the earth; a funnel cloud; Arizona's meteor crater; home video of a helicopter crash. And the face of Barbara Steele.

For more than 40 years, Steele's magnificent features and the intensity of talent that animates them have haunted the dreams of countless filmgoers and television watchers. She is, in a word, singular: tall and slender, with long raven hair and enormous, piercing eyes that suggest willfulness and intellect. Her cheekbones are pronounced, her mouth full and expressive. A strong chin dominates a square jaw.

She is considerably more than merely pretty, yet is not beautiful in the traditional sense. Without question, Steele is ferociously compelling. When she deigns to exhibit the spider's gaze she mastered years ago, we see perfection and imperfection, heat and chill, the intensity of life and the eternal darkness of the grave.

From her first starring film, *La Maschera del Demonio* (*The Mask of the Demon*; U.S. title, *Black Sunday*, 1960), in which she played a vengeful witch and the witch's innocent descendant, Steele has been typecast as a dark goddess, a stunningly beautiful yet malevolent creature capable of doling out pleasure and pain in equal measure.

Black Sunday was the first of many horror films Steele made in Italy. She took dual roles more than once, and even when she played but a single character, her persona suggested the extremes of female sexuality. Male viewers yearn for her even as some are intimidated. Females envy her power.

Paradoxically, Steele's ability to intimidate compounds her desirability. By the standards of Western society, where female sexuality is feared as strongly as it is desired, Steele is the *ne plus ultra* of the Eternal Feminine. Onscreen, she is a creature of wild extremes, the breathtaking beauty who inspires rapture and desire but whose price often is the immolation of the worshipper's body and soul.

The real Barbara Steele is not a dark goddess, and for many years she refused to discuss that aspect of her screen persona. Although she has worked with Fellini and Schlondorff, only the horror pictures interest most of those who came to interview her. These are films Steele made very quickly, sometimes simultaneously with others when she was very young. They helped her to learn her craft, but because their themes and aesthetics are weighted in favor of director and cinematographer, the films also frustrated her and left her feeling unfulfilled and even abused. So it is that this erudite, poetic woman came to be viewed as a completely different sort of creature, one quite inimical to the actress' true nature. And yet for all this, Barbara Steele's dark persona seems true; it certainly is meaningful, as it tells us volumes about our ambivalent regard for women and female sexuality.

Because the horror films Steele made in Italy revolve around archetypes—unprincipled scientist, victimized wife, malevolent succu-bus, stalwart hero—and rigid, codified settings and situations—dank castles, shadowed corridors, thunderstorms, torture, nightmares, death, resurrection, revenge—almost no one except the director, art director and cinematographer got to have fun. Less actors than symbols, the onscreen participants in *Nightmare Castle*—the dubbed, American-release version of the 1965 Italian thriller *Gli Amanti d'Oltre Tomba* (*Lovers from Beyond the Tomb*)—and similar thrillers were forced to perform within strict boundaries and conventions. Even Steele, who at least was able to exhibit wide ranges of emotion in her horror films, was asked to run through *the same range* in picture after picture. It was what audiences expected and, all the worse for Steele, it was a trick, an actor's stunt, at which she happened to be very skilled. Because she was young and wanted to work, she agreed to do the trick over and over again.

Steele described to film historian Mark A. Miller the "crisis energy" of a low-budget, short-schedule picture that propels the activity on the set and brings a flush of excitement to every participant. That energy is apparent in *Nightmare Castle*, which was directed by Mario Caiano (credited on American prints as "Allen Grunewald") in a

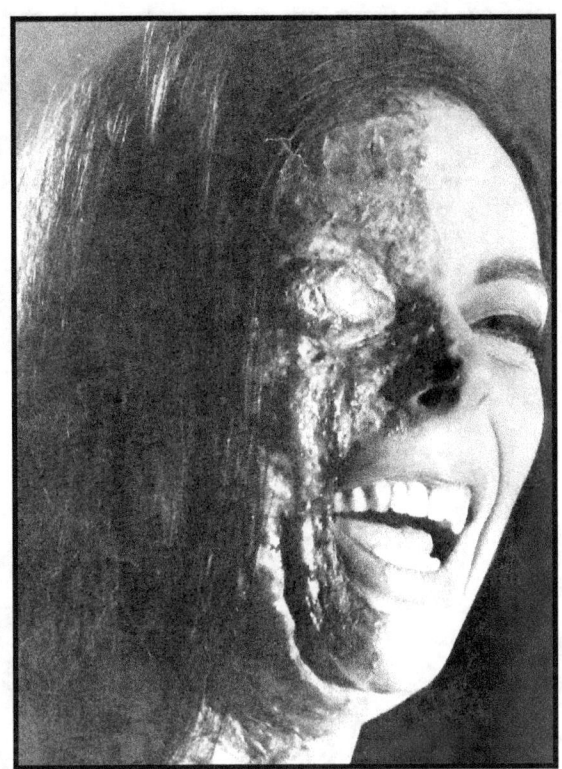

Barbara Steele, whose ferociously beautiful face is hidden by horrible, disfiguring makeup, cackles with evil in *Nightmare Castle.*

bluntly forceful style that is simpatico with the elemental story.

At Hampton Castle in an isolated part of England in 1872, Dr. Stephen Arrowsmith (Paul Müller) makes prisoners of his wife Muriel Hampton (Steele) and the gardener David (Rik Battaglia) after discovering them locked in an embrace in the castle greenhouse. Arrowsmith helps himself to a measure of Muriel's blood and transfuses it into the body of his aged housekeeper, Solange (Helga Liné), restoring her to beautiful youthfulness, thus allowing her to resume duties as his mistress.

Muriel's usefulness at an end, she and her lover are tortured by Arrowsmith and then murdered. Arrowsmith sears their hearts in flame, then buries the organs beneath a potted plant (which Solange solicitously waters). All seems well, except for one thing: Muriel has left her considerable estate to her mentally unstable stepsister Jenny, who is confined to an institution. The fortune that Arrowsmith desires will not fall into his hands as readily as he had hoped.

Nothing if not a pragmatist, Arrowsmith arranges for Jenny's release and marries her. Once installed at Hampton Castle, Jenny (Steele, in a long blonde wig) suffers frightful nightmares and visions conjured by her predecessor, who had sworn to Arrowsmith, "You can kill my body, but I'll never leave you in peace!" Jenny's mental fragility is all right with Arrowsmith, who is

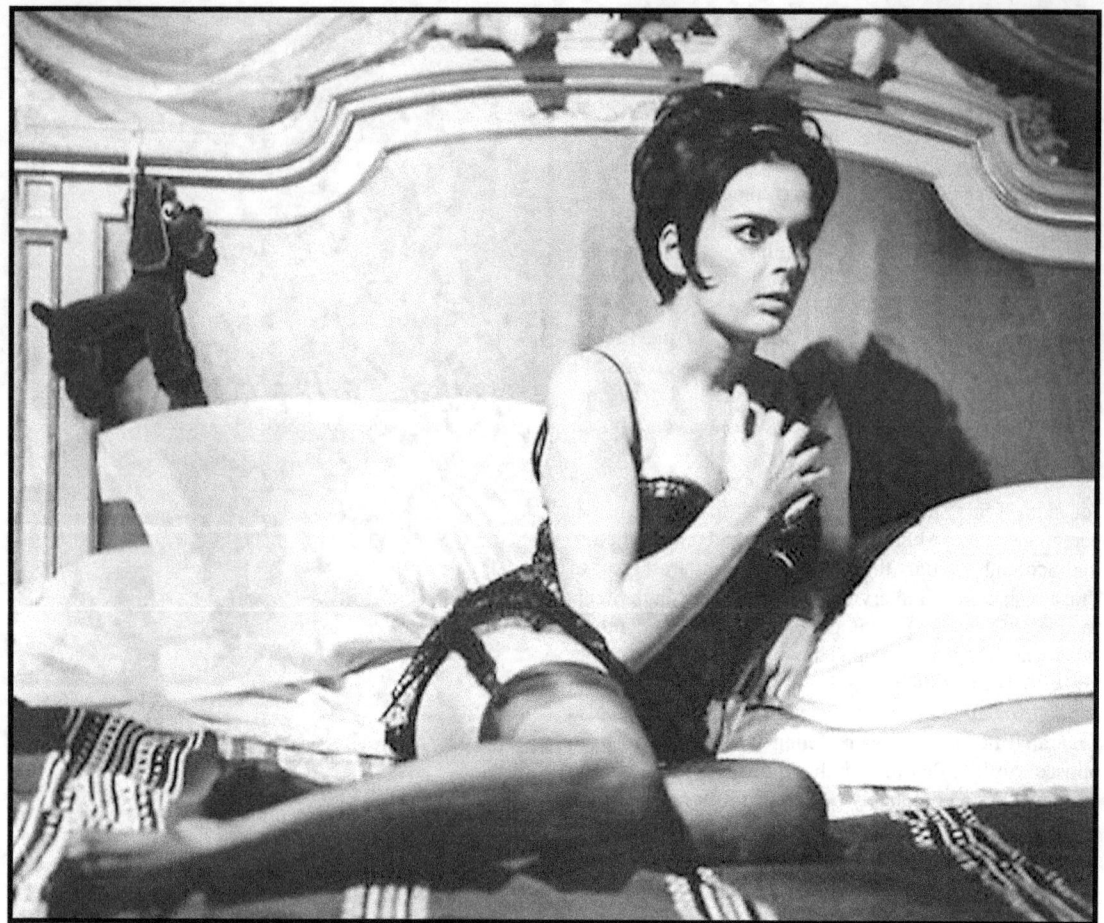

Barbaara Steele's horror movies revolve around archetypes—unprincipled scientist, victimized wife, malevolent succubus, stalwart hero—and in this typical Steele performance her icy, cold sexiness is apparent.

anxious to be rid of her. The jealous Solange, too, is eager to see Jenny disposed.

However, Arrowsmith's plans are threatened by the arrival at the castle of Jenny's handsome young physician, Dr. Joyce (Lawrence Clift). An attempt on the doctor's life misfires, and before Arrowsmith can try again, his crime against Muriel is revealed. At the climax, the dead are resurrected and Arrowsmith and Solange receive just punishments.

In a splendid article Steele wrote in 1994 for *The Perfect Vision* magazine, she asserted that "the best period of Italian horror films came out of the 1960s, when Italy was enjoying a carnival period of phenomenal optimism and the shadowy side surfaced with all of its attendant dark, beautiful, baroque, [C]atholic symbolism."

Nightmare Castle, while very much in this mold, is superficially amusing on some counts, notably the very Italianate look of the supposedly British Hampton Castle, and the perfect coincidence of Jenny's resemblance to Muriel (Jenny's blonde hair punches home the light/dark, good/evil nature of her relationship to her stepsister in an obvious but undeniably vivid manner). The English-language dubbing swings between good and awful. While an unidentified American-sounding actress dubbed the voice of Muriel, Steele (vigorously) recorded the English dialogue of the vulnerable, anxious Jenny.

The film is sobering because, like many other horror movies from the Continent, it suggests that the natural state of relations between men and women is warfare. From the opening scene, in which Muriel mocks Arrowsmith for his experiments and makes no secret of her infidelities, we understand that these two are on a collision course. If tenderness or even physical attraction ever existed between them, nothing remains now but hatred and disdain.

When Arrowsmith surprises his wife and the gardener in the greenhouse, he exhibits no sorrow, no regret, only a nasty sort of pleasure at an opportunity to punish and humiliate. "You don't know yet how long it takes to die of pain," Arrowsmith promises, with emphasis on the word "yet."

Inside the castle, Muriel and David undergo the tortures of the damned. They are manacled to a wall, whipped, dribbled with acid and finally cuffed to a bed, where they are electrocuted in a darkly parodistic sequence in which "marriage bed" and "deathbed" become one. But the last laugh, the disposition of the Hampton fortune, is Muriel's.

Solange, learning that the estate will go to Jenny, fixes Arrowsmith with a deadly glare: "I wouldn't risk the gallows for so little. I want my share!" This male-female relationship, too, is grounded in greed and self-interest.

From the first scene with Jenny, *Nightmare Castle* explores the duality of the characters played by Steele. Physical and psychological parallels are quickly drawn between Jenny and her stepsister: views of a glowering portrait of Muriel are intercut with close-ups of Jenny's face. Jenny has nightmares in which she imagines herself in the greenhouse, embracing the gardener before being confronted by a faceless man. The script takes care to reveal that, although Arrowsmith had hoped to induce Jenny's nightmares with drugs, the drugs were never given. Jenny is dreaming entirely on her own. Arrowsmith is pleased—it means he will have an easier time driving his new wife insane—but he is apparently oblivious to the possibility that Muriel is making good on her threat.

The emphasis on duality continues. Jenny and Muriel are related, so Muriel's blood is Jenny's. It is fitting then that the voice of Muriel comes to Jenny in the night moaning about "My blood! My blood!" While this is going on, more of Muriel's blood is being transfused into Solange, an act that physically involves Jenny in Arrowsmith's adulterous relationship with Solange, and in his murder of Muriel.

Eventually, Jenny's personality begins to be subsumed by Muriel's. When Jenny enters Arrowsmith's laboratory and wordlessly slices her husband's cheek with a scalpel, it is (almost literally) Muriel who grips the blade. Although neurotic, Jenny is essentially good, so the fact that she is being overpowered by the vengeful nature of her stepsister is unnerving and horrific.

The visiting Dr. Joyce (who is, in effect, the flip side of Arrowsmith) is not truly important to the outcome of the central struggle for Jenny's mind and soul. Like Solange, he is merely a satellite that revolves around the larger forces of Arrowsmith and Muriel/Jenny. He's well meaning, but terribly slow to pick up on the dangerous turn of Arrowsmith's mind. It is ridiculously easy for Arrowsmith to auger a hole into the base of the bathroom wall and run an electrical wire to Joyce's tub; only happenstance, the butler's fatal decision to reach into the bathwater for a bar of soap spares Joyce's life.

By the time Dr. Joyce finally resolves to spirit Jenny away from the unhealthy atmosphere of the castle, Arrowsmith has other ideas. He has witnessed Jenny's innocent conversations with Joyce ("You forget that greenhouses are made of glass and I'm not blind!"), and

Barbara Steele's first starring role, as a witch, in *Black Sunday*.

now needs Jenny in order to keep Solange alive, because what remains of Muriel's blood is going bad. "That damn blood!" Solange complains. "It's turning to poison in my veins! Heavy, like mercury… I need pure blood. Jenny's blood!"

In a startling moment, Arrowsmith abruptly attacks Jenny when she enters the parlor, rendering her unconscious with chloroform and carrying her to the lab where Solange awaits the transfusion. While this goes on, Hampton Castle (in the best Gothic tradition) shudders beneath a violent thunderstorm.

The sharp visualizations of duality continue: Two women lie on lab tables. Twin tubes are ready for the transfer of blood. The Hampton crest—twin hearts—dominates the family crypt (where the snooping Dr. Joyce discovers Muriel's sepulcher to be empty).

When Joyce discovers Muriel's buried heart and pulls a scalpel from it, the disfigured Muriel and David appear as phantoms, first beneath an arch on a balcony above Joyce, and then very near to him. The ghosts knock him unconscious and prepare to carry out their vengeance. The undead Muriel confronts Arrowsmith in the lab, gripping his hand and allowing herself a bit of pedantry that links the physical body with emotion: "You can't destroy flesh, any more than you can destroy love or hate. It's all the same thing."

Arrowsmith makes prisoners of his wife Muriel and the gardner David from *Nightmare Castle*.

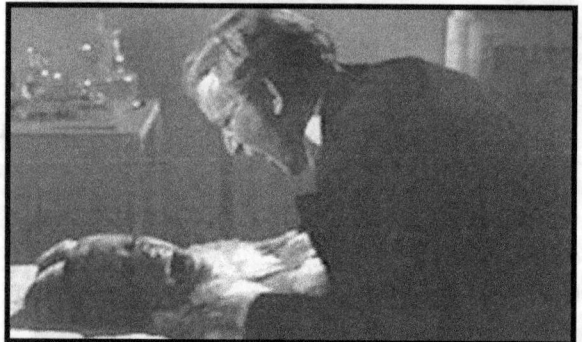

Arrowsmith attacks Jenny, suggesting the natural state between men and women is warfare; *Nightmare Castle*.

The phantom gardener slashes Solange's forearm, and her blood—Muriel's blood—courses onto the floor. Simultaneously, there is a sympathetic flow of blood from Muriel's hand to Arrowsmith's.

Muriel taunts Arrowsmith with her scarred face, maneuvering him into a chair (a contraption with mechanical, immobilizing arms) and setting him ablaze with a kerosene lamp. (Subsequent close-ups of the juicily sizzling corpse are eye-opening.)

The camera dollies in on Solange's head, by now a rotted skull, and cuts to a dolly-out from Muriel's ravaged face. One of Muriel's alter-egos has been destroyed, and Jenny is next on Muriel's hit list. She is saved from death only when the revived Dr. Joyce retrieves Muriel's heart and tosses it into the blazing fireplace. In an instant, both phantoms are gone.

Director Mario Caiano and cinematographer Enzo Barboni clearly had fun during the shoot and probably were not nearly as exhausted as Steele, who spends almost the entire picture in states of fury and hysteria. Sequences of Jenny's nightmares are particularly impressive, dominated by intense close-ups on Steele's wide eyes and what Jenny perceives to be the wildly swinging ceiling and chandelier above her bed. Steele stares, tosses and moans like one possessed.

Most interiors are cleverly lit as if from a single source, giving a painterly, chiaroscuro effect that is at once richly dramatic and oppressive. ("Italian cameramen," Steele has written, "grow up immersed in an awareness of light. It is a part of their mythology.") Steele's face, a marvelous construction of planes and angles, is shown to splendid, almost overpowering advantage. In this film, as in most of her other starring vehicles, Steele transcends mere humanness to enter the rarefied realm of icon and pure emotion.

Interestingly, vulnerable fright is one emotion that Steele expresses with particular force, notably during Jenny's dream of the greenhouse. Caiano chose to shoot the sequence without sound and in stark overexposure that gives a "hot," grainy look reminiscent of the dreamlike sequences in Carl Dreyer's 1932 classic *Vampyr*. In addition, the actors simulated slow motion, which is somehow an eerier effect than had the camera been overcranked.

When Arrowsmith interrupts the couple's embrace, his face is obscured beneath a tight stretch of white gauze, giving him a foreboding, ghostly aspect. Ennio Morricone's piano-dominated minuet score, emphatically passionate in other moments, is subdued and keening here and gives the sequence added tenseness and anticipation. When the faceless intruder begins to beat the gardener, Jenny abruptly awakes, unsure of what the images mean but aware that she has stumbled into something horrible that is not her doing, but for which she is likely to suffer, nonetheless. The film tells us that when the unprincipled are motivated by dark sexuality and brute emotion, the innocent inevitably suffer.

Mario Caiano was an assembly-line director on the order of Jess Franco and Riccardo Freda, though he was neither as prolific (or as exploitative) as Franco nor as artful as Freda. But like them, Caiano was adept at directing hysterical subject matter and bringing it in on schedule and on tight budgets. (A typical shoot during Steele's Italian-horror period was less than two weeks, and often filled with 14- and 18-hour days that she described as being "charged with Sambuca and coffee.")

The main burst of Caiano's activity was in the 1960s, though he remained active well into the 1970s and possibly beyond. His other directorial credits include *Ulisse contro Erole* (*Ulysses Against the Son of Hercules*, Italian-French, 1961); *Maciste, Gladiatore di Sparta* (*Maciste, Spartan Gladiator*, Italian-French, 1964); *Per Piacere, Non Sparate Col Cannon* (*Please, Don't Fire the Cannon*, Italian-Spanish, 1965); *Los Espias Mantan en Silencio* (*Spies Kill Silently*, Spanish-Italian, 1966) and *La Svastica Nel Ventre* (*The Swastika in the Womb* aka *Nazi Love Camp 27*, *Living Nightmare*, 1976). On English-dubbed prints of the last-mentioned film, Caiano is credited as "William Hawkins."

Barbara Steele was the last person signed as a contract player by the Rank Organisation, Britain's dominant filmmaker/distributor for a quarter of a century. Steele was given small roles in such trifles as *Bachelor of Hearts* (1958) and *Upstairs and Downstairs* (1959) before her contract was sold to 20th Century-Fox in

1960. She was subsequently assigned to co-star in a Don Siegel/Elvis Presley Western, *Flaming Star*, but fled to Europe when Hollywood-style moviemaking and the requirements of the role angered and frustrated her. That same year Italian director Mario Bava cast her in a dual role in his horror masterpiece, the aforementioned *Black Sunday*.

From that point it was off to the races as Steele worked steadily for the next nine years, appearing in Federico Fellini's *Otto e Mezzo* (*8 1/2*, 1963); *Le Monocle rit Jaune* (*The Monocle*, 1964, a spy comedy); Volker Schlondorff's *Young Törless* (1966, one of her best roles, as an oversexed beauty who initiates a young male student in the ways of the world); *Honeymoon with a Stranger* (1969, an American TV-movie)—and a plethora of horror thrillers: Roger Corman's *The Pit and the Pendulum* (1961, for many years, Steele's sole American feature); Riccardo Freda's *L'orrible Segreto del Dr. Hichcock* (*The Horrible Dr. Hichcock*, 1962) and its sequel, Freda's *Lo Spettro* (*The Ghost*, 1962); Antonio Margheriti's *La Danza Macabre* (*Castle of Blood*, 1963); Margheriti's *Il Lunghi Capelli Della Morte* (*The Long Hair of Death*, 1964); Camillo Mastrocinque's *Un Angelo per Satana* (*An Angel for Satan*, 1965); Massimo Pupillo's *Cinque Tombe per un Medium* (*Terror Creatures from the Grave*, 1965); Michael Reeves' *Il Lago si Satana* (*The She Beast*, 1966) and Vernon Sewell's disappointing *Curse of the Crimson Altar* (1967, American-release title *The Crimson Cult*).

Barbara Steele's cheekbones are pronounced, her mouth full and expressive.

Steele also worked in episodic television in the early and mid-1960s, "guest-starring" on *Alfred Hitchcock Presents*, *Adventures in Paradise*, *Secret Agent* and *I Spy*. Most notable of her later TV appearances is a fine performance in a 1972 episode of *Night Gallery*, "The Sins of the Fathers."

Steele married Oscar-winning screenwriter James Poe in 1969, gave birth to a son in 1970 and went into semi-retirement. She was divorced from Poe in 1974 and returned to features, but now as a full-fledged cult actress recruited for showy roles in an odd mix of films that included Jonathan Demme's *Caged Heat* (1974, as the crippled warden of a women's prison); David Cronenberg's *They Came from Within/Shivers* (1975, as a lesbian whose kiss infects her female neighbor with a strange, slug-like parasite); Joe Dante's *Piranha* (1978) and a foolish slasher thriller called *Silent Scream* (1980). In addition, Steele took supporting roles in *I Never Promised You a Rose Garden* (1977) and Louis Malle's *Pretty Baby* (1978).

Following a stint as a script reader for MGM, Steele joined Dan Curtis Productions as associate producer of the mammoth 1983 TV miniseries, *The Winds of War*. She put her film experience and multilingual skills to good use, scouting locations and interviewing actors. Steele moved up to VP/producer status for the follow-up miniseries, *War and Remembrance* (1988). In 1991 she co-starred in a brief TV revival of Curtis' *Dark Shadows*. Today, the actress, slender and strikingly attractive in her 60s, divides her time between Los Angeles and Europe.

The opening credits of TV and video prints of *Nightmare Castle* are restricted to the film's title and the names of Barbara Steele and Allen Grunewald. The closing credits comprise a complete cast list, but no production information is given and no behind-the-scenes personnel are listed. Casual viewers will be left mystified as to the particulars of the film's creation.

And in one of those quirks of marketing that bedevils film historians, *Nightmare Castle* has been released at various times, in various nations, under a plenitude of titles. As noted, it played in Italy as *Gli Amanti d'Oltre*

Barbara Steele is, in a word, singular: tall and slender, with long raven hair and piercing eyes.

Tomba; in Britain it was *The Faceless Monster*. Other titles include *Night of the Doomed* and the none-too-subtle *Orgasmo*.

As *Nightmare Castle*, a 90-minute cut of the picture, released by Allied Artists, played American theaters on July 5, 1966. Effective poster art was dominated by a stark artist's portrait of Jenny, with complementary figures of the undead Muriel and David, and a castle exterior (not the one seen in the film). Ad lines were bluntly exploitative: "A MAD, SADISTIC SCIENTIST ON THE LOOSE!" "WARNING! See it with someone who's shockproof!"

The print made available to television by Allied Artists ran 83 minutes—seven minutes less than the U.S. theatrical print. In 1980 Hollywood Home Theatre released an 82-minute version on video.

Two important reference sources, Walt Lee's *Reference Guide to Fantastic Films, Vol. 2*, and *The American Film Institute Catalog: Feature Films 1961-70*, note an Italian-version running time of 105 minutes, while *Video Watchdog* magazine claims 97 minutes. Whichever is correct, it's apparent that at least seven minutes and possibly 15 minutes of footage exist that never were part of any cut with the *Nightmare Castle* title.

In a major 1966 review marking the film's release in France, *Midi-Minuit Fantastique* writer Frederic Vitoux described Steele as "fascinating and macabre," and noted the way in which the male-female conflict that dominates the opening sequence gives the film "an immediately violent sensibility." Vitoux also explored what he called the "double" aspect of the Steele persona, observing that while Muriel is a creature of "violent eroticism," Jenny is "indecisive, hesitant, disoriented, [and thus] vulnerable."

Over time, *Nightmare Castle* has come to be regarded, with *Black Sunday*, as the quintessential Barbara Steele vehicle and as perhaps the finest record of her beauty and remarkable screen presence. Still, latter-day critical reaction has been ambivalent. *The Encyclopedia of Horror Movies*, edited by Phil Hardy, describes the picture as "less a horror film than a well-intentioned, but bad, love poem addressed to Steele… The film seems frozen in its fetishistic contemplation of [her]…" Hardy's companion volume, *The Film Encyclopedia: Science Fiction*, calls the film a "sadistic melange of Science Fiction [sic] and horror," adding, "Steele is in fine form as the avenging sister, and some of the sequences are powerful… A capsule comment in a 1973 installment of *Castle of Frankenstein* magazine's "TV Movieguide" (likely written by Joe Dante or Bhob Stewart) describes *Nightmare Castle* as "strong, heavy stuff—perhaps not for the queasy," and adds, "Highly recommended." Leonard Maltin's *Movie and Video Guide* calls it a "typically atmospheric European horror film," and notes the "good photography." An unidentified contributor to the book *The Horror Film* wrote that the picture is "a worthwhile effort for [Steele]… *Nightmare Castle* finds its greatest success in showing the beautiful horror icon in as many extreme situations and personas as possible."

Extreme is an apt summation of the horror-film portion of Barbara Steele's career. Her ambivalence about this body of work is understandable; she has stated more than once, for instance, her desire to do comedy or to play "a housewife in a scruffy cardigan." Steele has found it difficult—and probably tedious, as well—to grapple with iconographic status, an intellectual conceit that has been foisted on her by others and that has no relationship to her real life. But like Robert Wadlow, the tallest man who ever lived; like the astonishing young Bardot; like

Barbara Steele's remarkable face and intensity of demeanor liberated her from anonymity.

the heart-stopping beauties of mythology, Steele has been cursed by nature. Her remarkable face and intensity of demeanor liberated her from anonymity, allowed her travel and a career and associations with fascinating people, but these same features also imprisoned her within severely limited emotional and stylistic boundaries.

The screen struggles to contain her power. No casting director would have dreamed of hiring her to play a mousy clerk or Gidget; Steele's reaction to being cast as a cowgirl opposite Elvis Presley was nothing if not sharply self-aware. Her 35-year search for a canvas large enough to accommodate her suggests that the horror film—with its requisite melodrama, violent sexuality and wild emotion—was a natural and perhaps inevitable stopping place. Regardless, Steele's career readily encourages "what if?" speculation. She would have been a potent Mary Todd Lincoln, for instance, a deliciously unexpected *farceur* à la Kay Kendall, an intensely watchable heroine of a film by Michael Powell or Rainer Werner Fassbinder.

In the end, of course, reality is what it is. *Nightmare Castle* is a good film of its kind and a compelling showcase for one of cinema's most potent and fascinating personalities. If we can take instruction from the nature of Steele's horror film roles, if we can interpret her performances in the larger contexts of our own lives, relationships and the cultures that produced them, then Barbara Steele's career has not been imprisoning at all, but a thing of vigor, honesty and liberation.

An Italian movie poster for *Nightmare Castle*

For Barbara

CREDITS
Producer: Carlo Caiano; Director: Allen Grunewald (Mario Caiano); Screenplay: Mario Caiano and Fabio de Agostini; Cinematographer: Enzo Barboni; Editor: Renato Cinquini; Art Director: Massimo Tavazzi; Set Designer: Dino Fronzetti; Music: Ennio Morricone; Costumes: Mario Giorsi; Assistant Director: Angelo Sangermano. A Cinemat/Produzione Cinematografica Emmeci film; Released in the United States by Allied Artists July 5, 1966. Black and White; 90 minutes; American TV print: 83 minutes; American video-release print: 82 minutes; Original cut running time: 105 or 97 minutes

CAST
Barbara Steele (Muriel Arrowsmith; Jenny Arrowsmith); Paul Müller; billed as Paul Miller (Stephen Arrowsmith); Helga Liné (Solange); Laurence Clift; billed as Lawrence Clift (Dr. Derek Joyce); Rik Battaglia (David); Giuseppe Addobbati; billed as John McDouglas (John)

SOURCES

Dietrich, Christopher S. with Peter Beckman, "The Barbara Steele Interview," *Video Watchdog* #7, September-October 1991

Fliegelman, Avra L., ed., *TV Feature Film Sourcebook*, Broadcast Information Bureau, 1978
Hardy, Phil, ed., *The Encyclopedia of Horror Movies*, Harper & Row, 1986
Hardy, Phil, ed., *The Film Encyclopedia: Science Fiction*, Morrow, 1984
Krafsur, Richard P., *The American Film Institute Catalog: Feature Films 1961-70*, R. R. Bowker, 1976
Lee, Walt, *Reference Guide to Fantastic Films, Vol. 2*, Chelsea-Lee Books, 1973
Maltin, Leonard, ed., *Movie and Video Guide 1996*, Signet, 1995
Miller, Mark, "Not Just a Horror Film Actress, Thank You!," *Midnight Marquee* #44, Summer 1992
Mulay, James J., ed., *The Horror Film*, Cinebooks, 1989
Nash, Ray Robert and Stanley Ralph Ross, *The Motion Picture Guide Index A-J*, Cinebooks, 1987
Steele, Barbara, "Cult Memories," *The Perfect Vision* #23, October 1994
"TV Movieguide," *Castle of Frankenstein* #20, Summer 1973
Upchurch, Alan and Tim Lucas, "Barbara Steele Videography," *Video Watchdog* #7, September-October 1991
Vitoux, Frederic, "Les Amants d'Outre Tombe: Un Onirisme Violent," *Midi-Minuit Fantastique* #15/16, December 1966–January 1967

FRANK STRAYER
POVERTY ROW'S DARK DIRECTOR

BY KENNY STRONG

In the period 1931-36 when Hollywood was running a monster factory and profitable business, dozens of horror and mystery films were produced yearly. As we know, this massive output ranged from the big-budget spectacles of Universal and MGM to the small-budget pictures of the independent Poverty Row film studios, which would turn out productions in days. In such a ripe era for classic terror, it may surprise readers that the most prolific horror director of the time was not James Whale, Tod Browning, Michael Curtiz or Karl Freund, but the always-anonymous Frank R. Strayer, who during the Golden Age helmed nine horror/mystery films.

Very little seems to be known about the personality and character of Frank Strayer. Because he didn't work often at the big studios, and when he did it was on B productions, he is not well remembered. He was a true journeyman director—shooting 84 films in 27 years—but one can see something more in his films than simply getting all the principals together and pointing the camera at them. The more web sites visited, and the more reviews of his films read, the more we see that Strayer's films are described by critics and fans as surprisingly good, or as interesting little films. Never really is the director himself analyzed, and that's what I hope to do here. In today's analogy, it was as if he were a television director, churning out episode after episode and garnering little credit for the quality he instilled in his work. Due to the popularity of his *Blondie* series alone, his direction was conclusively an instrument for success.

Along with the *Blondie* films, Frank Strayer is perhaps best remembered for directing a series of Poverty Row horror films in the 1930s, most notably the ever-present and accessible quasi-classic, *The Vampire Bat,* starring Lionel Atwill. Nine horror/mysteries, most available on DVD and in the public domain, will be examined. One must realize too when viewing these forgotten films that he/she is seeing poor 16mm prints that likely fail to convey what the camera originally captured. What audiences will see, though, is a certain quality of character and common themes that run consistently through Strayer's work. Strayer created a sense of horror that really represents what I see as a sort of median level of what 1930s' Golden Age horror encompassed as a whole. He used all of the conventions of the genre both ably and respectfully so. He always worked with the stingiest of budgets, yet always created an interesting film. Kimball Jenkins of the great Missing Link Horror Film web site said it best: "They say imitation is the sincerest form of flattery, and although many independent studios strived to equal Universal's best, only Frank Strayer came closest."

Strayer was born in Altoona, Pennsylvania on September 21, 1891. He attended the Pennsylvania Military

Academy and also Carnegie Tech after high school. In World War I he served as an ensign with the United States Navy and, upon returning from the war, he joined Metro as an assistant and second unit director. Reportedly he also worked as an actor, though records are sketchy here. He was married in this period to Erma P. Rogers and had a son, Frank Jr., in 1928. It is not known whether his son is still alive.

He began directing features in 1925 with a melodrama called *An Enemy of Men* for Columbia, but comedies ended up being his major focus in the silent era. Reaching perhaps his greatest industry buzz in 1927, he directed Clara Bow at the height of her fame in *Rough House Rosie*. Additionally, he helmed two Wallace Beery vehicles the same year—*Now We're in the Air* and *Partners in Crime*. All seem to be lost or too difficult to see today. As sound approached he veered away from comedies, making his first talkie in 1929—*The Fall of Eve*. At this time, he began picking up directing work at low-budget studios. Strayer shot many dramas in this period, including *Fugitive Road* in 1934 starring Erich Von Stroheim and *Sea Spoilers* in 1936 with John Wayne. It was in 1931, though, that he made his first mystery film.

FRANK STRAYER

"Steppin' Out"
"Sweet Rosie O'Grady"

NOW DIRECTING

CLARA BOW

in

"Rough House Rosie"

Based on his own story, and one of only two writing credits (along with *By Appointment Only*), he shot *Murder at Midnight*. This film has many of the elements that Strayer would revisit in his successive horror and mystery films. *Murder at Midnight* starred Aileen Pringle, who was a popular silent actress and whose other genre credit was the lead in Tod Browning's *The Mystic*. From the titles, the film opens with a close shot of a hand changing a clock to strike midnight and then the camera ominously prowls through a dark house. We find two men quarreling over a woman, Esme Kennedy (Pringle), and the husband shoots her male lover. The camera pulls out and reveals a crowd of people watching their friends act out this scene—a game of charades. However, when the lover, Duncan Channing, is found truly dead, the real murder mystery begins.

Before we the viewers or any characters in the film know what's going on, Mr. Kennedy is killed. Alone in his office, Mr. Kennedy promises the killer that he's left a hidden letter that would convict him. The killing is meant to look like murder-suicide, an open and shut case, but Inspector Taylor (Robert Elliott) comes to investigate and Walter Grayson is the prime suspect. Colton, the lawyer, tells also of how Mr. Kennedy changed his will before he died. Millie (Alice White), a tart of a maid, tries to blackmail Grayson into marrying her (his sister is Mrs. Esme Kennedy). Millie is then promptly murdered. The butler Lawrence, played by the always-welcome Brandon Hurst, finds the letter and the will while vacuuming, but before he can disclose the location of these items to the police, the phone line is cut and he too is killed. Montrose, a family friend, discovers that Lawrence was killed with a protruding needle in the phone that was released when he hit the contact. Esme's Aunt, Julia, finds the will and letter in the vacuum upon realizing what Lawrence was up to. Skeptical of the police, Julia rushes to Montrose's office to tell him of the secret letter, but Inspector Taylor is there to confront her and uncovers the murderer.

This is a well-written mystery that keeps audiences guessing and is logical in its conclusion. It's quite comparable in pace and tone to *The Black Camel*, a Charlie Chan film made by Fox the same year, only without *The Black Camel*'s larger budget. It is also a real hoot listening to Brandon Hurst announce each person as dead. He is inappropriately emotionless and cold—completely ignoring the feelings of those he's informing. He's excellent as is the rest of the cast. Some creative camera angles include an effective low angle from the floor late in the film when Montrose is surprised by Aunt Julia's shadow, she

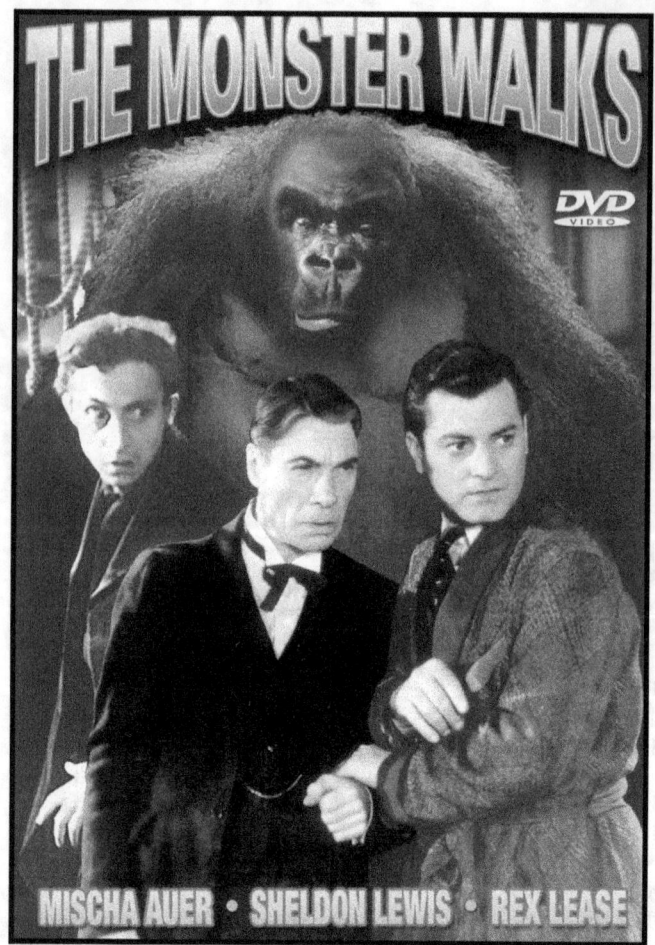

sequence is filmed as a perfectly mysterious low angle shot, and it sets the wonderfully moody tone for the film. Only seven characters appear in this film, plus an ape named Yogi. Some big bonuses include Martha Mattox playing her familiar sinister-looking housekeeper—this time named Mrs. Krug; Mischa Auer as her ill-tempered son, Hanns; and Sheldon "The Clutching Hand" Lewis playing the crippled elderly brother, Robert. Auer has a Lugosi-like evil to him, only without the bravura Lugosi would have brought to this role. The scene when he discovers his mother dead is a well-acted moment of shock.

The plot involves a man named Phillip Earlton who dies, and upon his death, a lawyer named Wilkes (Sidney Bracy) conducts a reading of his will. His daughter Ruth (Vera Reynolds), her fiancé Ted (Rex Lease), Ted's chauffeur (Willie Best), Robert, Mrs. Krug and Hanns are all gathered before the inevitable havoc is wrought. After they go to sleep the clock rings midnight and an ape's hand puts out a candle. The camera creeps in and tracks the heroine alone in her bed as the ape's hand comes from the wall behind her and grabs at her. This scene is straight out of *The Cat and the Canary*, Paul Leni's trend-setting 1927 classic. Smugglers originally inhabited the house, so secret passageways abound and paintings on the walls move eerily.

In terms of sound, Strayer uses it to his advantage. The thunder is effective as is an offscreen violin played by Hanns that adds to

holding a gun. When Aunt Julia runs to Montrose, the camera tracks along with her and creates a very tense scene. Audiences feel her terror and determination all at once. The ending is an example of very archaic American values. Rather than live with the shame of the murder and face trial, the murderer is given the opportunity by Inspector Taylor to commit suicide with his own device. The killer chooses to answer the phone and dies as a confession. Mild comic relief shines with the assistant cop constantly cracking peanuts, but this is a taut thriller that doesn't waste any time or scenes. As Strayer wrote the screenplay, it's interesting to see how many of these mechanisms return for his upcoming horror/mysteries.

The Monster Walks is one of the best known of Strayer's horror films. It was even given a VHS release from Kino Video way back in 1992. It is a film that's easy to criticize, as the film utilizes many old dark house clichés. To me, these aspects become assets of the film, but the lack of suspense is the true liability. *The Monster Walks* opens with a brilliant shot that is never quite matched again. We see a side view of a bed with a tall, lighted candle next to it as the curtains blow from the raging thunderstorm outside. The man lying on the bed is dead. The

the mystery. No other music is heard in the film. The ape here is no more dangerous looking than the one in Robert Florey's *Murders in the Rue Morgue* from the same year, but at least this ape looks more consistent than that of the other film. Comic relief comes from Willie Best as the chauffeur, who apart from enacting a stereotyped comic performance, gets to breathe the most life into the scenes he's in.

The Monster Walks differs from Strayer's other mysteries in that there are so few suspects other than the ape, so the movie is never as engrossing as one would hope. There are no subplots generated between other characters and this limits the suspense and adds to the slowness of the story. However, Strayer makes up for a lot of this with an intimate setting. Once again, murder occurs at midnight, as Strayer continues his clock motif. The difference between this and the previous film is that Strayer now seems to have been influenced by full-blooded horror films, *The Cat and the Canary* being chief among them. The mood is sustained throughout, which makes *The Monster Walks* a truly iconic representative of the old dark house period. However, this includes the best and worst aspects of the genre. The lack of character development and tired clichés are all here too.

Fay Wray and Lionel Atwill in Frank Strayer's *The Vampire Bat*

In *Tangled Destinies*, released by Mayfair Pictures Corp. in 1932, Strayer does a solid job of building suspense. And as he would do almost as frequently, he would dump the suspense in the end for an abrupt conclusion. This is one of those mysteries that simply does not provide any tangible clues as to the identity of the murderer, so audiences just have to wait it out. *Tangled Destinies* has the most intimate feel of any of his films. After the opening scene with the passengers leaving the plane, all the action takes place in just a few rooms in the spooky house.

The plot involves a plane transporting 13 people that's headed for Los Angeles and is forced to land in the desert to avoid a great storm. The flight number—in a nice touch—is 13. They reach a local uninhabited mansion and invite themselves to spend the night. As the characters get to settle in, the storm roars. Shortly afterwards, the lights go out. A man, Forbes, is missing and found dead. Sidney Bracy plays a professor who turns out to be an insurance inspector named McGinnis. McGinnis' company insured Forbes' stolen diamonds for $500,000. Some red herrings include a priest, an elderly lady and a Chinese gentleman named Ling. McGinnis finds the murder weapon—a broken tree limb. They resolve to search everyone for the missing diamonds and some of the passengers suspiciously object. It turns out the elderly woman finds the gems in her knitting bag, but they prove to be a fake. After various twists, the murderer is unveiled.

Once again no music exists to heighten suspense, only a plane's engine sounding over the opening credits. There's a good bit of offscreen dialogue, particularly as we watch the old lady sneak around the room to find the real diamonds. Vera Reynolds, the heroine from *The Monster Walks*, appears again. A silent screen actress, she would star in one more film for Strayer that year, *Gorilla Ship*, and then retire for good. James Leong as Ling is as humble as Charlie Chan, even after he is mistakenly attacked in the dark late in the film. The lack of familiar faces makes it hard to follow all 13 of these characters for the tight 64 minutes, but the script actually does a good job of trying to define each and give some background information before the plot starts spinning. The dialogue is better than average for a Poverty Row chiller and Strayer waits until halfway through the film to kill off a character. The standard subplot of a young lady who finds out her fiancé is a liar and drops him for the pilot is incorporated. This subplot is well balanced with the murder plot. Only the conclusion comes rather abruptly and isn't as satisfying as one would hope. The killer really comes out of left field—and beyond. *Tangled Destinies* is perhaps the most obscure of all Strayer's films.

The Vampire Bat, however, is probably the most well known and also the best of Frank Strayer's horror films. The plot is familiar to classic horror lovers, so I will dismiss discussing it. The cast is so good it really distinguishes this film from other Poverty Row thrillers. This is the complete opposite of *Tangled Destinies* in terms of cast as Strayer is given grade A actors who worked at the major studios when this film was made. How a small studio like Majestic cast all of them is the real mystery! Lionel Atwill was fresh off his horror debut in *Doctor X* and also the New York stage, where he ranked only behind John Barrymore in popularity during the 1920s. Fay Wray similarly just finished *Doctor X* and was about to star in the colossal *King Kong*. Melvyn Douglas had just finished acting on the same sets in James Whale's *The Old Dark House* and was at the beginning of an outstanding career that included two Academy Awards. The supporting cast is full of great horror genre veterans—Dwight Frye is Her-

Even Fay Wray, along with Lionel Atwill, looks sinister in *The Vampire Bat*, perhaps Frank Strayer's best-known horror film.

rific camerawork with many moving shots and good use of close-ups, which is an improvement over Strayer's previous horror films. In a suspenseful moment early in the film, the camera pans all around the room, ending on the old woman who is startled as a black cape cloaks around her. Once again, Strayer uses his theme for midnight when the first murder occurs. When Atwill's own maid is murdered, the cross is once again present—this time on the floor as the camera neatly pans and settles on it. The cross, used as a plot device, is a nice touch as the murderer uses it to pin the crimes on Herman. The cross also proves ineffective against this vampire.

In particular, Melvyn Douglas makes this film a cut above the rest. In the type of role that many hollow male leads would drown in, Douglas shows the difference a good actor can create with average material. He is compelling, charismatic and dramatically plays along with the action as one would want for this sort of fun. Atwill is solid throughout and is given one truly great moment—his mad doctrine to Fay Wray at the end. And Dwight Frye, who seems to let it all out here, has the best (and funniest) line in the film as he tells the frightened Maude Eburne, "You give me apple, now, Herman give you nice, soft bat." George E. Stone also has a great portrayal as the doomed Gringen.

The only true fault with *The Vampire Bat* is the conclusion. For all the care and mood Strayer imbues within this production, he leaves audiences with the disappointing finale. The fight takes place offscreen (á la *Dracula*) and is over instantaneously. The climax shows no real imagination and it is unimaginable why Strayer would allow this

man the village loony (*Dracula*); Maude Eburne plays the old woman comic relief (*The Bat Whispers*); William V. Mong is Sauer, the sniveling townsman (*Seven Footprints to Satan*); George E. Stone is Gringen, a local gossiper (*The Spider*); Lionel Belmore plays his patented Burgomaster, here called a Burgermeister (*Frankenstein*); and Robert Frazer is Emil, the innocent tool of the evil madman (*White Zombie*). Most are playing roles based upon stereotypes in American cinema. The superb casting and the use of Universal's sets truly make this film a model for anyone who wants to be introduced to the genre of classic horror films—both major studios and Poverty Row. This film almost represents a median level between the majors and the minors.

Majestic Pictures, headed by Phil Goldstone (*Murder at Midnight*), produced the film written by Edward T. Lowe (*Tangled Destinies*). There's plenty of classic horror imagery and trademarks in this film. A wolf howls as bats hover over the night and a mysteriously cloaked man leaps across the rooftops. The symbol of the cross appears, illuminated in the room of the old woman who is murdered early in the film. The torch-carrying villagers chase Herman in the traditional kill-the-fiend scenes through the German countryside, here doubled for by the California hills. The European village sets from *Frankenstein* are well used and are archetypal. The film also sports a mad doctor lab in a spare, but appropriately bleak, manner.

The music over the opening credits is archaically spooky in the best sense and shows up later in Strayer's other vampire tale, *Condemned to Live*. There's some ter-

In *The Ghost Walks* a tree tumbles, a bad storm rages and a well-dressed party of people must stay in a nearby house for the night.

after spending most of the film creating wonderfully suspenseful moments. Unfortunately, Robert Frazer is used mostly as window dressing for horror movie fans. His relationship with Atwill's doctor is the one relationship in need of enhancement, so the finale could have been more exciting. Curiously the film, like all the previous efforts by Strayer, ends on a single comic line that seems to disregard the overwhelming horrors.

Fifteen Wives, a 1934 release, is the one film this writer has not yet viewed. It seems to exist, but is extremely difficult to acquire as the usual sources such as Sinister Cinema's *Forgotten Horrors* collection do not contain it. George Turner and Michael Price did view a 16mm copy that was floating around when they wrote their landmark book *Forgotten Horrors* in 1979, but according to Price, it has since gone by the wayside.

The plot of this film is complex and concerns the murder of a bigamist who has, yes, 15 wives all around the world. The bigamist's name is Steven Humbolt, and upon his arrival in New York City, he is found dead in his hotel suite. A detective, Decker Dawes (Conway Tearle), comes upon the scene and the murder investigation begins. It seems three of the widows are in New York—an evangelist Sybilla Crum (Margaret Dumont), Carol Manning (Natalie Moorehead) and Ruby Cotton (Noel Francis). The latter two are re-married, although their new husbands know little of their checkered pasts. Humbolt also tried to blackmail Carol in his visit back to New York. As the investigation continues, small pieces of glass are discovered near flowers delivered to Humbolt. After sending the glass to the chemist (Robert Frazer), it turns out the killer used a poisonous gas sent in a small glass globe along with the flowers. The gas in the globe was released with sound waves, coming from a radio station playing a program starring "The Electric Voice"—who can shatter glass in certain instances. Also, Carol had an apartment in Philadelphia from which the poison was shipped. It turns out one of the Voice's associates is Ruby. But shortly after, Sybilla finds out that the florist who sent the flowers, Jason Getty (John Wray), has a secret regarding Mr. Humbolt, too. Sybilla is then killed and Dawes unveils the murderer in the exciting finale.

Plenty of suspects abound, and within a 68-minute running time, Strayer kept the action moving swiftly. And what a sardonic treat it would be to see Groucho Marx's famous foil, Margaret Dumont, in such a role—murder victim! Observing the film, Turner and Price stated, "Director Frank Strayer takes full advantage of the contrasting elements of humor and the macabre. Camerawork and cutting are innovative, with a constant sense of motion and considerable care in sustaining the viewer's interest as the story darts among its many principal players." We can only hope this missing piece of Strayer's work will shed its cinematic light upon us again soon.

Frank Strayer's affinity for comedy came through with his very deliberate spoof of the horror genre, *The*

Ghost Walks. Often very funny with a great sense of self-awareness, Strayer again shows that he not only respects the horror genre, but he is also aware of its limitations as well. The plot is a fun one. A writer, Prescott Ames (John Miljan), takes Mr. Wood (Richard Carle) and Erskine his secretary (Johnny Arthur) on a getaway weekend, but alas! A tree tumbles down in the road and a bad storm rages so the party is forced to stay in a nearby house for the night. At the house, Prescott has secretly hired thespians to act out the horror play he's written, in hopes of winning over Mr. Wood. Naturally, when one of the actors turns out to be really dead, they have a true mystery on their hands. The best part is when Mr. Wood and Erskine find out the secret shortly before Prescott discloses it to them. Figuring everything to be untrue, they still refuse to believe Prescott, despite his pleas. A guard (Spencer Charters) shows up and says a madman is loose on the premises. After a short while, it becomes clear that the madman is one of them.

The Ghost Walks becomes a cross between Paul Leni's *The Cat and the Canary* and *The Monster*, directed by Roland West, both of which were based on popular stage plays of the 1920s. Johnny Arthur even played the lead in *The Monster*. Strayer is clearly in his element here. Based on his *Murder at Midnight*, he shows that he is not simply interested in giving the audience a drawing room mystery. He wants to let the audience in on the secret with him, but he does this after first luring the viewer into a false story.

Maxine Doyle (Marguerite) and Ralph Morgan (Professor Kristan) from *Condemned to Live*

He then spoofs all the tricks of the trade from paintings on the walls with missing eyes to the roaring storm outside. His skill for comedy is given a purposeful turn in this film as it is not simply comic relief for straight horror—the movie is equally a comedy and a horror film. And best of all, the film provides a great opportunity for many of the actors to shine in their respective roles. Winning top honors is the teaming of Richard Carle and Johnny Arthur as the Broadway professionals who refuse to believe that each peril they face is legitimate. They play comedy for all it is worth and their performances prove a treat. Carle is so cynical and yet understanding, his character is comically well rounded. Arthur is the tart assistant, who mourns his own misfortunes, but he can still verbally hold his own against his oft-acerbic boss. And Charters gets to be so silly in the finale, audiences wonder what they were worried about earlier in the plot. *The Ghost Walks* is a fun little film, but is so clichéd as a mystery that if audiences saw either *The Cat and the Canary* or *The Monster*, the mystery of *The Ghost Walks* is solved instantaneously. *The Ghost Walks* may disappoint upon first viewing, but with repeated viewings it certainly garners appreciation. As a spoof, it shows Strayer's full awareness of his palette and merits his craftsmanship in not one but *two* genres.

Condemned to Live, made in 1935, is a much different animal, and is just as serious as *The Ghost Walks* is comedic. It opens with a dark scene in a cave with a young pregnant woman suffering. Her husband and friend Dr. Dupre (Robert Frazer) try to save her. The cave is infested with monstrous bats. Unfortunately, the men are too late as one bites her. We flash forward many years later to find a village, whose people have become overwrought with deaths that they believe are caused by a mysterious vampire. Professor Kristan (Ralph Morgan) is leading the pursuit of the fiend. However, we find out Kristan was the son of the pregnant woman, and he is doomed to a destiny as the unknowing vampire whose recent life stresses have caused the deadly change in him.

Condemned to Live is one of a handful of full-blooded vampire films outside of *Dracula* and *Dracula's Daughter* made in Hollywood in the 1930s. The film uses its sets to the fullest with lots of great props including candles, fireplaces, old bookcases, ornaments and elegant décor and costumes. Again, Strayer had use of Universal's back lot and prop department to film this vampire tale, and it's impossible not to compare this film to *The Vampire Bat*. The first thing that we notice is an absence of camera movement, and the movie is far slower-paced film as a result. The same skulking score is used, and most of all, the vampire theme is the strongest. However, this vampire attacks and kills his victims only when in the presence of searing rays from the moon. Our first experience is when Kristan wakes and suffers the plight of the moon's rays and kills his first victim. It's no mystery who the vampire is, so this time the story is meant to bring sympathy to the tortured soul. "Shun the dark," Kristan tells all the villagers. "Go home and guard yourself with light," he says. In a very effective shot, Marguerite's maid Anna opens the door and sees the vampiric Professor Kristan, and the strong wind instantly blows out her candle. In cinematic language, her death is now imminent. Marguerite is safe, though, as her candle never goes out. "We are well lighted," Kristan says as he tells Marguerite he has to break up their engagement. But being around the kindly Kristan, she confidently puts out the room candles that quickly anger him. Her ignorance puts her in danger as Kristan's true identity is awakened.

As stated above, this film is a strange animal. It is archaically written. The characters speak as if cast in a 19th-century stage play. Many outdated moments may induce laughter today such as the vampire snarling or Marguerite becoming frightened at the simple appearance of Kristan's hunchbacked assistant Zan. And it seems every member of this town worships Professor Kristan as a God on earth! On the other hand, the film is quite mature. There is a great awareness of the distinction of love and being in love by Marguerite, who agrees to marry Kristan for the sake of her father's wishes. And Strayer here seems to ignore the then-modern conventions of vampire films to create a film that is unique in how sympathetic and naïve a tale it is. It is fairy tale-like and completely innocent. *Condemned to Live* is as serious as a funeral, just as inversely *The Vampire Bat* took itself as pure pulp. Ultimately, Strayer intended this to be a sad story of a very sympathetic vampire and his faithful hunchbacked assistant. The acting is consistent with this and the film avoids the supporting comedy so often prevalent in these types of films. These qualities make it a most welcome addition to the 1930s horror genre and it is quite unique and satisfying on its own terms. The film seems a bit of an experiment from Strayer, who boldly gave up the safe comedy and created a vampire very different from the famous Count created by Bela Lugosi. His next film, changing form again, would be a traditional murder mystery.

Murder at Glen Athol is similar to *Murder at Midnight* in tone and atmosphere. John Miljan plays a detective named Holt who takes a vacation to write a novel. A neighbor, Muriel, invites him to a party she's having. Muriel has a lot of enemies. She's blackmailing a racketeer, fooling around and making everyone hate her. Naturally, she is a murder victim—but this time there's another murder, a man named Campbell. Still another man, Harry Randel, is shot on the roof as an intruder. Holt discovers that Campbell was struck on the head and not killed with the knife that lay next to him. Muriel is found in her bed, stabbed, blood covering the sheets. Holt also develops a romance with a woman named Jane, whom he met at the party. After the racketeer's men trap Holt, he finds out that Campbell gave the racketeer, Coletti, the knife. A big car chase scene ensues and Holt kills the racketeer's men. Nervous about his illegal affairs, Coletti killed Campbell to keep him quiet because Campbell found Muriel dead with the knife in her that he knew was Coletti's. The killer got ahold of Coletti's knife, but Holt does not make the arrest as Coletti's forced deathbed confession proves both murders. Holt and Jane then go on a cruise for their honeymoon. The killer—as revealed in a radiogram in the end—committed suicide out of guilt. *Murder at Glen Athol* is a complex little mystery with a very abrupt conclusion, which is not well explained.

The ending is so fast and confusing I had to watch it three times to figure out what I just saw. The film seems to be in such a hurry to end that the leading couple is off on the obligatory getaway before a satisfying resolution is even met! It is well constructed, though, and the identity of the killer is logical and motivated. Comic relief is provided by James Burtis as Holt's down-and-out ex-Irish boxer servant. The car chase scene mentioned is a rarity for Strayer, but it is fast paced and a nice change of pace from the usual goings on. As usual, the clues and deaths are quite odd and keep us on our toes. Happily, the mystery is not too unbelievable and ridiculous. It evolves realistically almost to the detriment of not being sensational enough.

John Miljan seems to on in cruise control in this film—a sort of second-tier William Powell. He's stolid, but shows some sharp wit toward his valet. Irene Ware, always beautiful but never too impressive as an actress, does just enough to earn good marks. The film was shot by M.A. Anderson, Strayer's frequent collaborator, who worked on 18 of his films between the years 1933-36. Robert Frazer has a supporting role, a veteran of eight Strayer films and many of these mystery/horror ones. Strayer does not indulge in the spooky elements with this film the way he did in *Tangled Destinies*, his previous mystery-oriented

film. He seems more influenced, perhaps, by *The Thin Man* films and similar detective films. It would be interesting to see how this film plays alongside *Fifteen Wives*. It's bright and often comedic; however, the murder moments are chilling, particularly the graphic scene of blood-soaked sheets—a scene handled quite nonchalantly. *Murder at Glen Athol* has the least horror content of Strayer's nine, but it's certainly entertaining with its detective-styled story, and it complements the other films nicely.

Last, but far from least, we come to *Death From a Distance*—Poverty Row's answer to Universal's *The Invisible Ray*. In some ways it is a better film than the Karloff-Lugosi picture. Sure, Karloff and Lugosi are missing and there's nary a note of music, but this swift looking detective film has an interesting mystery plot and great atmosphere. It involves astronomy, which gives this potboiler a fresh approach. And next to *The Vampire Bat*, it's Strayer's most entertaining horror/mystery film.

A group of scientists gather in an observatory for a lecture by the famous Professor Einfeld (Lee Kohlmar). No sooner than we are dazzled by the wonderful special effects of the night sky, a shot is fired and Dr. Stone is murdered. Detective Mallory (Russell Hopton) arrives on the scene along with a reporter, Kay Palmer (Lola Lane), who was covering the lecture. There are many worthy suspects in the audience, all of whom are questioned by Mallory. Despite the enclosed setting, the murder has been cleverly committed and Mallory releases the suspects, save a Hindu (John Davidson) who is secretly being held for illegally entering the country. Kay is frustrated with Mallory, who is against her reporting any of this story for fear of the case getting out of hand. She defies him and uses his dim-witted assistant Regan (Lew Kelly) as a source for an exaggerated story. She unknowingly puts Professor Einfeld's life in danger, however, and Mallory is now forced to come up with a plan to save the Professor and reveal the killer. Mallory finds a clue that leads him to believe the Professor will be murdered in the observatory at the time he will observe the star Arcturus. He finds a contraption that will automatically fire a gun when Arcturus is in line with the coordinates of the observatory's giant telescope. Resetting the gun, he sets up the killer to confess after faking that the Professor was really murdered by the killer's weapon.

Death From a Distance is a neat mystery with solid suspects and a novel, impressive planetarium setting. The special effects are terrific and were accomplished by Jack Cosgrove, one of the best in the business who would go on to work on many classics including *Gone With the Wind* and *Prisoner of Zenda*. *Death From a Distance* makes use of the same Universal set for *The Invisible Ray*. The film opens and closes with nice pan shots, one to set up the murder, the other to set up the hero and heroine hooking up in the finale. Even in the worn print, the lighting is attractively done. As Strayer's done in previous films, he includes plenty of details, such as blinds in the windows of office rooms—the type of addition to the film's compositions that makes them more visually interesting. Overall, like many previous Strayer films, the production looks more expensive than it probably was and here Strayer takes strong advantage of the astrological aspects of the story. It's an ingenious murder concerning the use of the star Arcturus. Even better is the final setup by Mallory. One by one he interrogates and releases the suspects he has gathered, building toward a tense conclusion. And this time Strayer ends with a bang—literally and figuratively. As weak as some previous murder revelations have been, this one is fully satisfying as is the light comic touch in the end wrap.

Looking back at the fate of this director and his being relegated to mostly B films for the duration of his career, a quote from silent screen star Louise Brooks may explain Frank Strayer's scenario during his early Hollywood years:

> As a director became powerful or established, the producers started to think of ways to get rid of him. After a director got so big that he could defy the producers, and demand a certain cast and budget, he was given a bum picture, and thrown out of the studio. With all the pictures sold in advance, it didn't matter if some were bad. I made three pictures with directors who suffered fear and agony, being forced to direct, that I dreaded going to the set to watch their struggles…in those days a writer was not much more than a means of getting a film down on paper, so it could be budgeted, cast and put into production. Frank Strayer had also been a writer. Most of the time such directors stood behind the camera letting the cameraman, Menjou, or Beery handle the direction.

The Strayer film she referred to is *Now We're in the Air* with Wallace Beery and Brooks. As for Strayer being a writer, he doesn't have any official industry writing credits before 1931. However, what she says is consistent in that Strayer was at an industry and commercial height in 1927 that he would not reach again. He was in his third year of directing and obviously up and coming. Did producers at Columbia and Paramount keep him down? It is possible, but being on Poverty Row gave Strayer a freedom he therefore may not have enjoyed at the big studios. And perhaps that's how he wanted it.

What may be more interesting are the seemingly different sections of Frank Strayer's career. He started out doing light, silent comedies in 1925. When talkies came around in 1929, he worked mostly in dramas. His horror/mysteries all came from 1931-36, and he directed a series of Spanish language films from 1933-35. In the year 1937 he directed four *Jones Family* comedies. From 1938-43, 14 of his 16 films were *Blondie* pictures and after a couple more low-budget films, he settled down in the late 1940s directing five religious-themed movies. He did only one other mystery film in his career, called *I Ring Doorbells* with Anne Gwynne for PRC in 1946. He seemed to shift or was shifted by the studios to specialize in certain types of films for certain periods of time. His last film, *The Valparaiso Story*, was released in 1951. Strayer retired from film directing and allegedly directed some television in the 1950s. Frank Strayer died at the age of 72 in Hollywood on February 3, 1964.

Frank Strayer's respect for the genres he worked in becomes the bottom line conclusions of critics after watching the Strayer Nine. As a horror film director, he indulged in all the trappings that horror fans wanted and expected. What today may seem like old clichés—such as the fear of the number 13, murder and mayhem taking place at the stroke of midnight, clutching hands emerging from secret passages, old-fashioned superstitions, villagers carrying torches to storm the feared monster and murderers being uncovered in a drawing room setting—were given not only a respect but a vibrant life from this director. Frank Strayer's horror/mysteries define both the strengths and weaknesses of classic horror. His Golden Age horrors are a major part of the support beam that holds high the treasured films fans have enjoyed for years. It's high time we pay tribute to the working man whose skillful direction at the ground level help define the genre as it is known today.

Notes: Special thanks to Harry Long; Les Adams; Charles Silver at MOMA; kind wishes to Michael H. Price and for the information provided from that wonderful stalwart of reference and entertainment, *Forgotten Horrors: The Definitive Version* by George E. Turner and Michael H. Price.

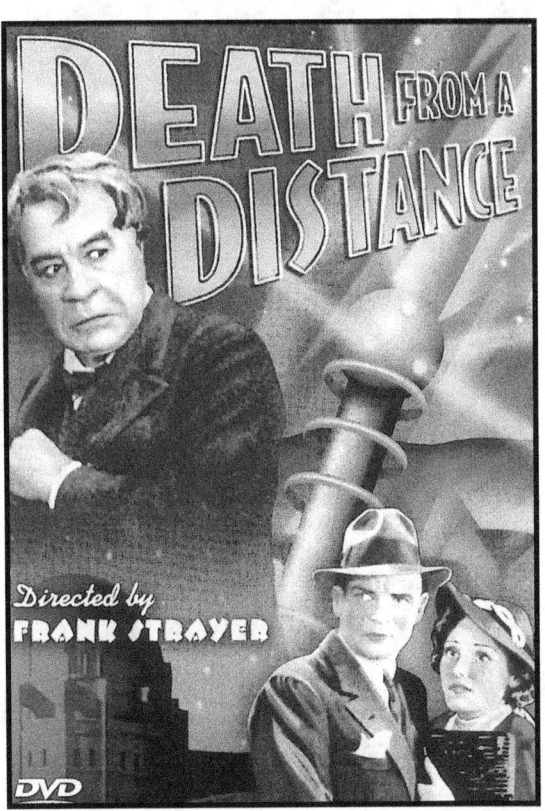

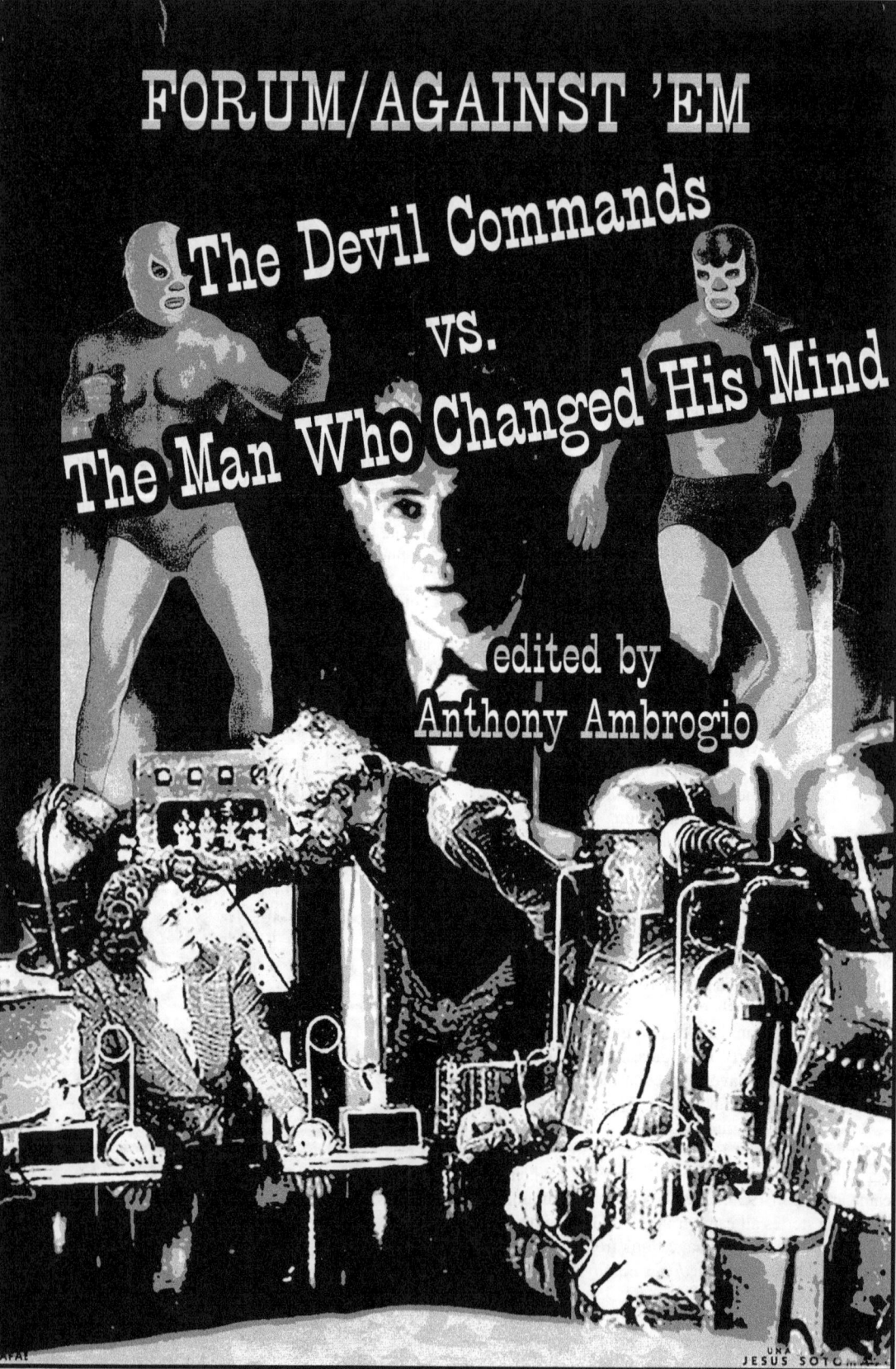

Gary J. Svehla (**GS**) wrote (in *Midnight Marquee* 71/72) about the relative merits of recently DVD-released *The Man Who Changed His Mind* (1936; U.S. title: *The Man Who Lived Again*) and *The Devil Commands* (1941), little realizing that he would provoke a firestorm of controversy among the magazine's regular contributors. First Mark Clark (**MC**) and James J.J. Janis (**JJ**) started in on him. It wasn't long before Anthony Ambrogio (**AA**), Arthur Joseph Lundquist (**AJL**), and Steven Thornton (**ST**) joined the fray, by which time the debate moved off into some surprising directions. Luckily, Bryan Senn (**BryS**) was there to bring the discussion back to its beginnings. [*Spoiler alert*: If you don't want to know what happens at the end of *The Man Who Changed His Mind* or *The Devil Commands*, don't read this article!]

GS: As I wrote in my DVD review for the summer 2004 *MidMar*, I think people will over-react and over-praise the merits of *The Man Who Changed His Mind* simply because the film has been nearly lost. It does look gorgeous, but the soundtrack is thin and very, very hissy! You won't notice the hiss until now that I mentioned it, and now that's all you will hear. Karloff is great, and his performance is one of his best.

Boris Karloff is great and his performance is one of his best in *The Devil Commands*. Everyone in the production lets his or her hair down and rocks out.

compare the film to *The Devil Commands*. I prefer *The Devil Commands* because everyone in it lets his or her hair down and just rocks out. *The Devil Commands* is a superior B production. *The Man Who Changed His Mind* is a tad more formally Brit, pretentious and stiff upper lip. Also, one of *The Man Who Changed His Mind*'s major flaws is that, although during the course of the movie every major player gets to imitate some other major player, *Karloff does not*. When his character's mind is changed into another body, he dies before he has the chance to imitate anyone. And, as I said, *The Man Who Changed His Mind* is so *veddy* British. For me, *The Devil Commands* is the better film. I prefer Karloff's performance therein. It's more natural and haunting. It touches me emotionally. The vacant look on Karloff's face speaks volumes.

MC: *The Devil Commands* is very good but not quite as well executed, overall, as *The Man Who Changed His Mind*. *The Devil Commands*, generally, has a haggard look about it.

GS: I have to disagree here. Karloff's haggard look is the basis for a first-rate performance. First of all, let's compare directors: the superb B-film director Edward Dmytryk for *Devil*, Robert Stevenson for *Mind*.

JJ: Stevenson is a criminally underrated director. I'd put him up against Dmytryk—whose batting average fell precipitously in the 1950s. Not so Stevenson.

[Dmytryk's directing career from its commencement to 1959: *The Hawk* (1935), *Television Spy* (1939), *Emergency Squad* (1940), *Golden Gloves* (1940), *Mystery Sea Raider* (1940), *Her First Romance* (1940), *The Devil Commands* (1941), *Under Age* (1941), *Sweetheart of the Campus* (1941), *The Blonde From Singapore* (1941), *Secrets of the Lone Wolf* (1941), *Confessions of Boston Blackie* (1941), *Counter-Espionage* (1942), *Seven Miles from Alcatraz* (1942), *Hitler's Children* (1943), *The Falcon Strikes Back* (1943), *Captive Wild Woman* (1943), *Behind the Rising Sun* (1943), *Tender Comrade* (1943), *Murder, My Sweet* (1944), *Back to Bataan* (1945), *Cornered* (1945), *Till the*

In a moody well-lit photograph, Anna Lee and Boris Karloff look concerned in *The Man Who Changed His Mind.*

End of Time (1946), *So Well Remembered* (1947), *Crossfire* (1947), *Obsession* (1949), *Give Us This Day* (1949), *Mutiny* (1952), *The Sniper* (1952), *Eight Iron Men* (1952), *The Juggler* (1953), *The Caine Mutiny* (1954), *Broken Lance* (1954), *The End of the Affair* (1955), *Soldier of Fortune* (1955), *The Left Hand of God* (1955), *The Mountain* (1956), *Raintree County* (1957), *The Young Lions* (1958), *Warlock* (1959), and *The Blue Angel* remake (1959).]
[Stevenson's directing career from its commencement to 1959: *Happy Ever After* (1932), *Falling for You* (1933), *Tudor Rose* (1936), *The Man Who Changed His Mind* (1936), *The Two of Us* (1936), *King Solomon's Mines* (1937), *Non-Stop New York* (1937), *Owd Bob* (1938), *The Ware Case* (1938), *Young Man's Fancy* (1940), *Return to Yesterday* (1940), *Tom Brown's School Days* (1940), *Back Street* (1941), *Joan of Paris* (1942), *Forever and a Day* (1943), *Jane Eyre* (1944), *Dishonored Lady* (1947), *To the Ends of the Earth* (1948), *I Married a Communist* (1950, aka *Woman on Pier 13*), *Walk Softly, Stranger* (1950), *My Forbidden Past* (1951), *Johnny Tremain* (1957), *Old Yeller* (1957), and *Darby O'Gill and the Little People* (1959)—plus episodes of the TV series *Gunsmoke*, *The 20th Century-Fox Hour*, *Alfred Hitchcock Presents* (all 1955), and *Zorro* (1957).]
MC: Stevenson was a perfectly capable craftsman. In fact, until the emergence of Steven Spielberg, he was the top-grossing director of all time, thanks to his series of hit comedies made at Disney in the 1960s—things like *Mary Poppins*.
[Stevenson's unbroken streak of Disneyana, which began with the aforementioned *Johnny Tremain*, *Old Yeller*, and *Darby O'Gill*, lasted for almost 20 years: *Kidnapped* (1960), *The Absent-Minded Professor* (1961), *In Search of the Castaways* (1962), *Son of Flubber* (1963), *The Misadventures of Merlin Jones* (1964), *Mary Poppins* (1964), *The Monkey's Uncle* (1965), *That Darn Cat!* (1965), *The Gnome-Mobile* (1967), *Blackbeard's Ghost* (1968), *The Love Bug* (1968), *My Dog, the Thief* (1969, TV), *Bedknobs and Broomsticks* (1971), *Herbie Rides Again* (1974), *The Island at the Top of the World* (1974), *One of Our Dinosaurs Is Missing* (1975), and *The Shaggy D.A.* (1976).]

He's best remembered for those films, but Stevenson was a bit more versatile than those movies would suggest, and he displayed a flair for the Gothic with his 1944 *Jane Eyre* (starring Orson Welles). I'm not knocking Dmytryk, who was more of a stylist than Stevenson and made some superb films, but Stevenson was no hack.

Under Stevenson's direction, the supporting performances in *The Man Who Changed His Mind* are very strong. Not so *The Devil Commands*.
GS: I'll take the blacklisted stylist over the mainstream hit maker any time! How can you say that the supporting performances are not as strong? The unsung Anne Revere as the charlatan spiritualist and Karloff's partner submits one of the finest female genre portrayals of the 1940s. She is utterly outstanding—creepy, strong-willed—and she always draws our attention to her. Her performance is simply fabulous—one waiting to be rediscovered.

Donald Calthrop as Clayton, the bitter old cripple, along with chain-smoking Boris Karloff, from *The Man Who Changed His Mind*

MC: I don't know if I'd go *that* far, but she is certainly very good. Unfortunately, hers is the *only* memorable supporting performance in the film.

GS: The dim-witted Karl, played by Ralph Penney, is oddly charismatic. He's almost so real that his performance doesn't seem like a performance. But he is quirky and quite effective.

MC: I'm not nearly as impressed with Ralph Penney as you are.

AA: I wish they could have cast Lon Chaney, Jr., in that role. He would have been a natural, and it would have made the picture better—more iconic.

MC: Be honest, Anthony. You wish they had cast Lon Chaney, Jr., in everything! You probably would have been happy if they'd cast him in the Anna Lee role in *The Man Who Changed His Mind*!

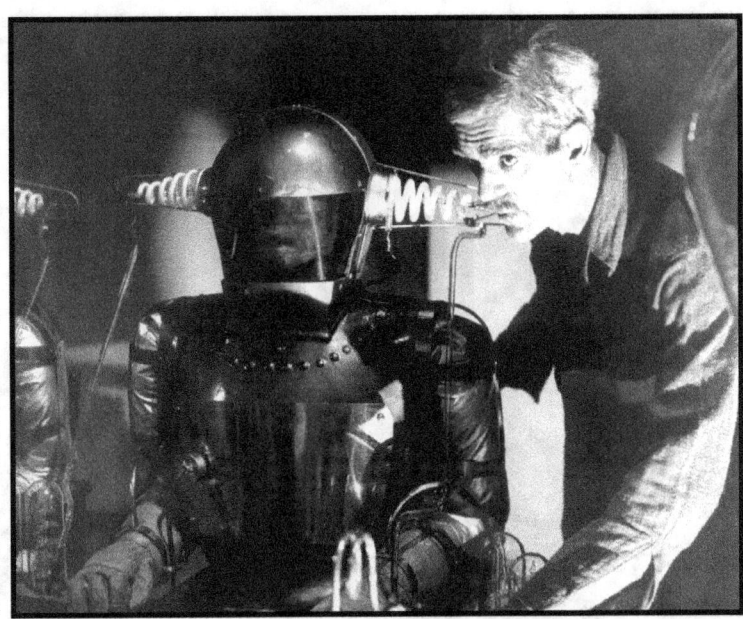

Boris Karloff, posing with his machines that allow him to communicate with the dead, looks corrupted by evil from *The Devil Commands*.

Speaking of which, *The Man Who Changed His Mind* has *three* great supporting performances: Anna Lee, who's terrific as the heroine; Frank Cellier, as Haselwood, the self-serving wealthy "philanthropist"; and Donald Calthrop as Clayton, the bitter old cripple who inherits Cellier's body. Cellier is even better once he begins playing Clayton-as-Haselwood.

GS: But, come on, does Karloff change his hairdo in *The Man Who Changed His Mind* like he does in *The Devil Commands*? The evolution of his coiffure from a slick combed-down look to weird curls actually makes the performance (as visual metaphor).

MC: You got me on that one.

ST: "And the Oscar for Best Hair Stylist goes to..."

GS: I find *Mind* a little too stiff and stuffy. *Devil* is fun all the way, with excellent supporting performances and superb direction by Dmytryk. It is my favorite Columbia Karloff. I can watch *The Devil Commands* over and over but *The Man Who Changed His Mind*, to me, does not lend itself to repeated viewings.

AJL: Need I add that Gary used to play *The Devil Commands* at Andover High at lunch times?

MC: I will grant that Karloff's character in *The Devil Commands* is much more sympathetic and, well, *Karloffian* than his character in *The Man Who Changed His Mind*. But *The Devil Commands* isn't my favorite Karloff Columbia mad-medico flick—that would be *The Man They Could Not Hang* (1939). However, I believe all three of these are very good films. I'm not sure any one is decidedly better than the other two. I've always liked *The Man Who Changed His Mind* best, *The Man They Could Not Hang* next and *The Devil Commands* third, but my margin of preference between each is small.

AA: Reluctantly leaving aside Lon Chaney, Jr., for a while, I wonder if it's not too far-fetched to suggest that *The Devil Commands* and *The Man Who Changed His Mind*, in different ways, foreshadow Karloff's later *The Sorcerers* (1967), directed by Michael Reeves, in which an old man (Karloff) and his wife (Catherine Lacey) practice mind control, à la *The Man Who Changed His Mind*, to vicariously, virtually feel younger people's experiences (sex, drugs, murder—this *was* the 1960s, after all)—and in which the woman, à la *The Devil Commands*, exerts greater and greater control over the man even as the experiment spins out of control.

The difference, though, is that, in *Sorcerers*, the experiment succeeds, and we get to see what happens. The thing I remember most upon first viewing *The Devil Commands* as a pre-teen is my frustrated disappointment that the movie ended before anything really happened. You know what I mean? Karloff is becoming more and more obsessed, setting up his experiment to talk to his dead wife; the preparations are becoming more and more elaborate and alarming, and—in the end—*nothing happens*. He gets interrupted. He dies. The end.

JJ: Karloff is *supposed* to be interrupted. He is about to go somewhere no one should go. If he got there, a whole can of worms would have been opened.

AJL: I go to the movies to see cans of worms opened.

ST: Yes, but Columbia couldn't afford a whole can of worms—only a night crawler or two.

AA: I'm with Arthur and the worms: That's why we watched these movies—to see the guy "tamper in things best left alone," to revel in the dire consequences, to be scared by resurrected dead bodies, vampires, spirits returning from the grave, etc. Not to be tantalized and frustrated. Does anybody else feel this way?

MC: Absolutely. If you want to be tantalized and frustrated, go to a nudie bar!

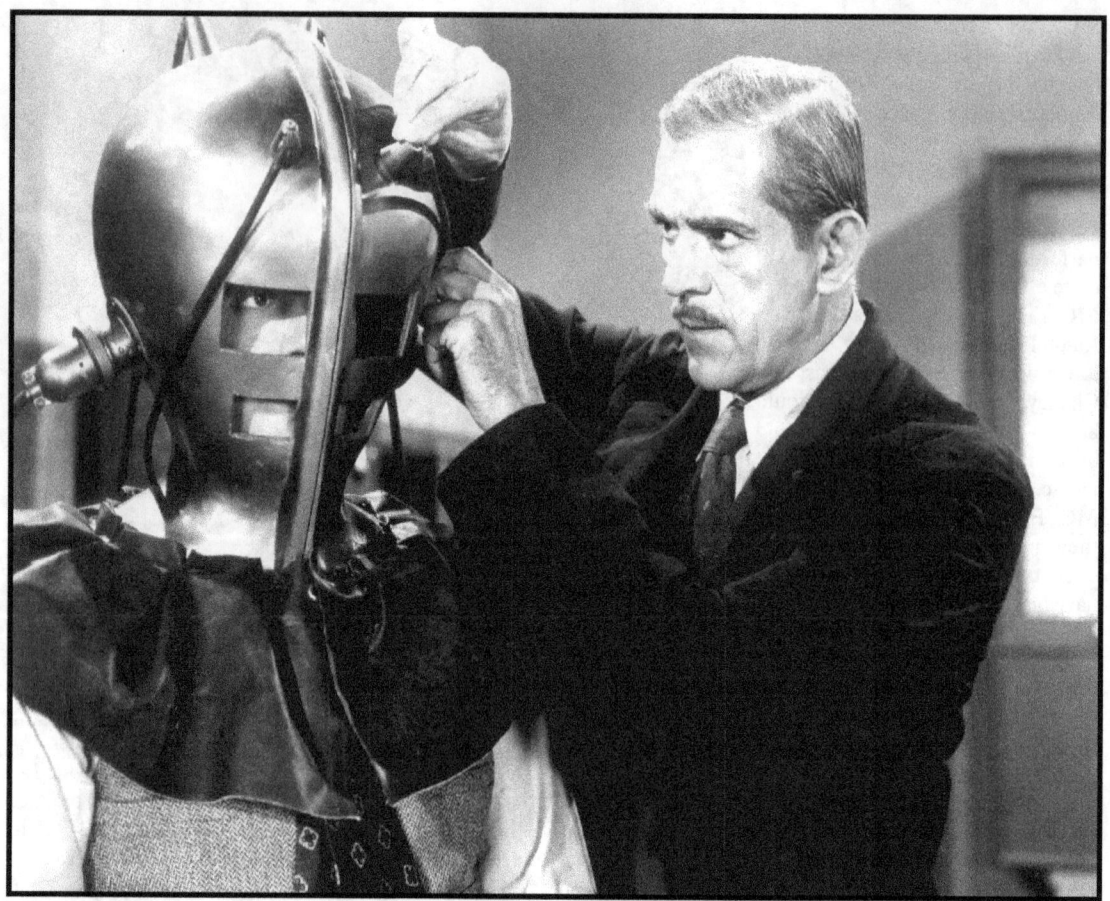

Boris Karloff, armed with his army of corpses, attempts to speak to the dead in *The Devil Commands*.

JJ: But the Invisible Man does *not* succeed in conquering the world. Frankenstein does *not* succeed in breeding a new race. Moreau does not succeed in creating the perfect humanimal and breeding it with a real human. Because there are things man must leave alone, and the Lord our God is a jealous God. One might as well criticize a Western because everyone rides horses...

AA: At least we got to see the Invisible Man *be* invisible. The movie didn't stop with the authorities arresting him just before he was about to take monocaine.

AJL: If *The Invisible Man* had worked like *The Devil Commands*, Griffin would have died just as his body first began to turn transparent, and the movie would have ended right there.

AA: Frankenstein *did* create a monster. The movie didn't stop with Elizabeth, Professor Waldman and Victor persuading him to give up his mad experiment and not throw the switch.

AJL: If *Frankenstein* had worked like *The Devil Commands*, Henry Frankenstein would have died just as his Monster first began to move, and the movie would have ended right there.

AA: And Moreau *did* create a whole bunch of manimals (and a womanimal) before everything came crashing down on him in the House of Pain.

AJL: If *The Island of Lost Souls* had worked like *The Devil Commands*, what's-his-name would have died just as his first animal began to mutate, and the movie would have ended right there.

ST: Yet, in *The Devil Commands*, Karloff's character does come tantalizingly close to realizing his goal. You can actually make out his wife's voice before the final-reel tempest destroys his lab.

AA: And then it all ends. Why couldn't he have made contact? Why couldn't the plot have progressed from there (along lines similar to/different from *The Walking Dead* [1936], maybe)? Why did it have to end before it began?

AJL: Once more, Anthony, we are of a single mind. Or, should I say, a single brain. All of these former films dare to actually let their anti-heroes "tamper in things best left alone" and let us get to see them experience the consequences of their actions.

Or, put another way, those movies have the guts to actually open the can of worms that *The Devil Commands* politely won't.

GS: The same argument can be made, as I stated earlier, for *The Man Who Changed His Mind*. The movie ends before the Karloff character gets to mimic, his mind literally changed, another character. But the movie is what it is, and I accept that.

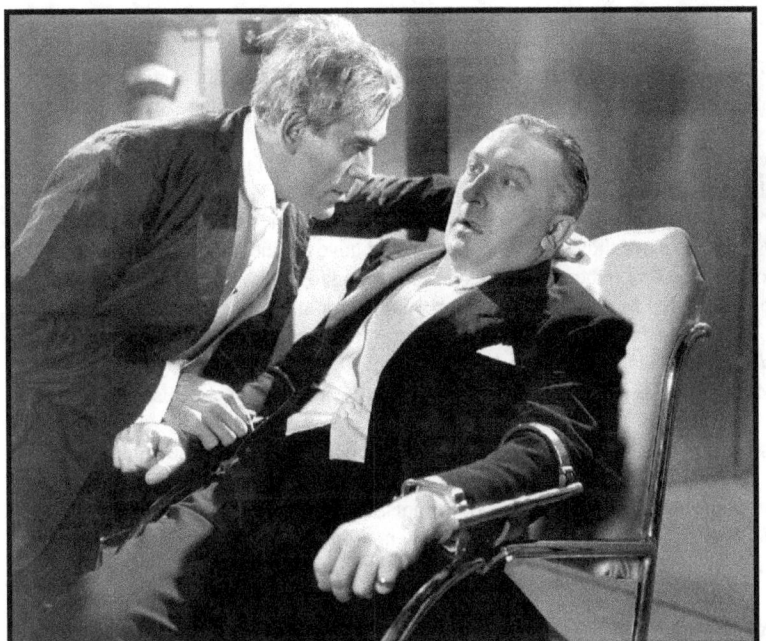

Boris Karloff attends to Frank Cellier, as Haselwood, before he switches his mind with that of a cripple from *The Man Who Changed His Mind*.

JJ: But that can of worms doesn't open because there are some things that man cannot do. If I remember correctly, the implication is that God basically said no. It is one thing to transgress against the laws of God and Man (and eventually pay the price). It is another thing entirely to storm the gates of Heaven... that probably goes a way toward explaining the film's title. Karloff may be a good man, but it is the devil that prompts him.

AJL: *The Devil Commands* goes nowhere because its jealous God slaps down its transgressor before he actually accomplishes anything. For me, that is a scriptwriter's cop-out, and the result is a very unsatisfying film in spite of the abundant talents of all involved. Dmytryk's *Captive Wild Woman* (1943) has less on the ball, but actually delivers a helluva lot more.

GS: But, Arthur, *The Devil Commands* does deliver the goods. Karloff's character does contact the dead, and his experiments succeed. What about the major sequence where the machine is activated and all the corpses, dressed in their metallic best, all lean inward as the crazed Karloff proudly stands at his command post? Things do happen here abetted by exciting visuals!

Where could the movie have gone... what do you see as the next-stage cop-out? The film builds into the explosive storm *in the laboratory* and ends in a whirlwind of fury. My heavens, what more can a B programmer deliver, Arthur? This is an exciting, thrilling conclusion.

AJL: Oh, hell, Gary, Karloff is trying to break down the wall into the realm of the dead. Remember, he's got a whole tableful of corpses right in front of him. The newly liberated spirits of the dead would inevitably take refuge in the bodies, bringing them back to life. But the spirits, having been driven mad by the shock of death, would be screaming, pain-filled madmen. Maybe competing spirits would battle for possession of bodies. Karloff, perhaps assisted by the spirit of his dead wife, would be forced to open the celestial vortex again and send them back into death. There could even be some kind of moral about how the Earth is the home for the living, as Vera Brittain writes in her autobiographical account of WWI, *Testament of Youth*: "If the living are to be of any use in the world, they must always break faith with the dead."

The Devil Commands tempts us throughout the entire film with the idea that Karloff is going to pierce the barrier between the world of the living and the world of the dead. When he finally does, the movie simply ends. It is all build-up and no delivery. I demand delivery. I demand closure. I demand cans of worms be opened!

JJ: Oh—so Blofeld *should* have started WWIII in *You Only Live Twice* (1967)? So Ygor and Boehmer *should* have taken over the state in *Ghost of Frankenstein* (1942)?

Boris Karloff as Dr. Laurience addresses an assembly of his medical peers who ridicule his work in *The Man Who Changed His Mind*.

The Monster and the Bride *should* have mated and created a new race? Jekyll *should* have been successful in separating the evil in men's souls chemically? Regardless of how films may be today, one must take into account how films were then. There were certain places where one could go and then pay the price, and there were those where one paid the price for even the attempt. Lovecraft was big on the latter as well. There are simply places where men are forbidden to go. *The Devil Commands* is about one of those places. God said no. That is the crux of the film. One either goes with that, or one fails to comprehend the film. *The Walking Dead* is similar.

BryS: I disagree. *The Walking Dead* has, well, a walking dead. The film *begins* with Edmund Gwynne breaching the barrier he was not meant to breach, and then segues into the consequences/issues that arise after such a breach. *The Devil Commands* is all about the *striving* for such a breach (which is, in itself, a valid dramatic story, giving Karloff some choice emoting opportunities). But they are very different films in terms of structure. Oh, and *The Walking Dead* is a helluva lot better as well.

JJ: Except Gwynne, in *The Walking Dead*, breaches the barrier to find out what is on the other side and fails. The Lord our God *is* a jealous God.

AA: I know what you're getting at, James, but you misunderstand me, I think. The thrust of the Bond film is different from *The Devil Commands*. In *You Only Live Twice*, we have the forces of good confronting the forces of evil—lots of action and intrigue, etc.—and, in the end, the good guys win before the bad guy can destroy the world. Nothing dissatisfying or frustrating occurs there.

I'm afraid I don't understand your Jekyll/Hyde example because Jekyll *does* succeed in separating the evil in men's souls chemically. The film shows us what happens when Jekyll becomes Hyde—how evil can take over a man's body and soul and lead to devastation and ruin.

As for your other two examples—well, again, we'd already been given the sense of wonder and had a chance to wallow in supernatural satisfaction before *Bride of Frankenstein* (1935) and *Ghost of Frankenstein* (1942) came to an end. However, if the movies had been longer, and if the filmmakers would have deigned to show it, it would have been really interesting to see what would happen in a state ruled over by a mad (or at least very cranky) scientist and a monster with the brain of a vengeful hunchback. Ditto a world of little monsters.

I understand that the "limits" established in the Golden Age were different and probably more narrow than they later became. I agree that sometimes the moral of a movie prevents Man from Tampering in God's Domain.

ST: Good points, Anthony. I've long felt that classic horror was the film genre most obsessed with God and morality, in spite of the many times it flirted with blasphemy.

AA: James mentions *Walking Dead*, as I did, and that's certainly the message in the end. However, at least we get to *see* Karloff as the walking dead, an inadvertent avenging angel of death, before the finale.

AJL: *The Devil Commands*' ending is where the movie should *start*. All it would take would be a screenwriter who was not afraid of actually exploring the ideas he brings up.

GS: No, no, no! Arthur, the focus in *The Devil Commands* is upon the scientist, his transformation from kind, nurturing husband to obsessed, deadly scientist who will violate any code to bring his dead wife's spirit back. The radical change in appearance (not just hair styles) Karloff undergoes only reinforces the point. This movie is character driven and is about how one's scientific obsessions can turn him evil. The movie is not about the product of his experiments. The movie's ending is satisfying, to me, because we clearly see how the altruistic Karloff character is destroyed, from within, having been seduced by the dark side. The plot is almost Shakespearean in structure.

BryS: Very convincing argument, Arthur. *The Devil Commands*' ending is indeed an abrupt letdown. But the film is not a total loss, due to its macabre topic and creepy atmosphere (and Karloff, of course). But yes, it could have (and *should* have) been a helluva lot more.

AJL: We are in complete agreement. I never said *The Devil Commands* was a total loss. Otherwise,

Boris Karloff and Anne Revere from *The Devil Commands*

I'd never be able to watch it to the end. It just lacks that zing at the finish that would carry it over into mythology. Movies with a helluva lot less to offer, like *The Unearthly* or *Invasion of the Saucer Men* (both 1957), manage in their final moments to give truly haunting spins on their central ideas and almost make the films worth sitting through.

For that matter, *Bride of Frankenstein* doesn't go on very long after the creation of the She-monster, but in that short time it manages to touch all bases satisfyingly.

ST: *The Devil Commands*' script may be no great shakes, but this movie delivers the goods in terms of atmosphere far more effectively than most B movie programmers of the era. Plus it has a couple of very fun performances.

Captive Wild Woman, on the other hand, always struck me as one of the least entertaining of the Universal Bs. Even with the presence of Carradine and some lively stock footage, this film seems dull as dishwater to me. I've never understood the minor cult surrounding it. Enlighten me, Arthur. What is it about this film that works for you?

AJL: Well, first, just in terms of comparison with *The Devil Commands*, I'd probably agree that *The Devil Commands* is perhaps better put-together technically than *Captive Wild Woman*. However, *The Devil Commands* is one of that breed of movies that makes me climb the walls, a movie that promises the world and then declines to deliver.

Captive Wild Woman, however, is about a mad scientist who wants to transform an ape into a woman. The movie goes on to present that very event and runs a few variations on the idea before it ends. Had *Captive Wild Woman* been structured like *The Devil Commands*, we would have ended up with something like *Sssssss* (1973), which is another film that makes me climb the walls, because we spend the whole damn picture waiting for the guy to get transformed into a snake, and, when he finally does, the movie suddenly terminates.

So that is why I'd rather sit through competent B-movie *Captive Wild Woman* rather than more-than-competent B-movie *The Devil Commands*.

Now, just in terms of itself, *Captive Wild Woman* does have a wonderful performance by John Carradine. In my article about the Paula the Ape Woman series, published years ago in *Midnight Marquee* and entitled "Universal's Poverty Row," I went on at length about a wonderful scene between Carradine and Fay Helm where Carradine shows a lot of subtlety and a delicious sense of evil. Acquanetta is pretty if fairly vapid, and the rest of the cast is just adequate.

Boris Karloff and Ralph Penney from *The Devil Commands*

Captive Wild Woman's main attraction for me is that it is not just a gland movie (*The Monster Maker* [1944]), not just a brain transplant movie (*Ghost of Frankenstein*) and not just an ape movie (*White Pongo* [1945]), but a gland-transplant, brain-transplant, ape movie with deliberate sex appeal. The film splices together all four of the ways in which pulp writers pondered the question of human identity after Darwin made us question whether we are divinely different from the animals, and, if its threads never really add up, at least they are there to play in our imaginations as we remember the film (which for me accounts for much of my enjoyment of any movie). And in my case at least resulted in an unpublished gland-brain-ape novelette.

JJ: *The Devil Commands*, *Captive Wild Woman*: For the record. I like both.

MC: You must have skipped *Jungle Woman* and *Jungle Captive*, then!

ST: Truthfully? I'd put them all on the same rung of the ladder—ground level.

AJL: Well, *Jungle Woman* is in a jaw-dropping basement all its own.

MC: *Captive Wild Woman* has that wild-and-woolly, anything-goes mentality going for it (sort of like a Silver Age DC comic book), an enjoyably over-the-top performance by Carradine and a hilariously inept one from Acquanetta. It's silly as all get-out, but it moves fast and is quite a bit of fun if you're in the right mood. *Jungle Woman*, however, is probably the dreariest, most lifeless hunk of junk Universal released during the 1940s. *Jungle Captive* recaptures some of the loopy fun of the original. It's passable.

JJ: I like all three Paula Dupree movies. I do not understand how anyone who professes affection for Ingmar Bergman or *Grand Illusion* (the illusion being that anything is actually happening) can criticize the Ape Woman trilogy.

Anna Lee and Boris Karloff in *The Man Who Changed His Mind*

MC: Funny. I can easily understand how someone who enjoys *Jungle Woman* might not be able to grasp the appeal of Bergman and Renoir.

JJ: *I demand a Dupree DVD set now!* I would be willing to do the commentary. Besides, in the bad-Universal sweepstakes, as long as the 1941 *The Black Cat* exists, everything else is just an also ran…

AA: You're just jealous because the 1941 *Black Cat* has a better cast than all the Ape Woman films combined—

JJ: Two words, Anthony: Hugh Herbert.

AA: If only Lon Chaney, Jr., had played the Broderick Crawford part in *The Black Cat*!

GS: Arthur, your suggested extended ending for *The Devil Commands* would make a fine movie, but, within the confines of a B programmer, could it be accomplished in another 15-20 minutes or so? If we had to cut out stuff from the beginning, we would lose a lot, including much of the Karloff character's disintegration—which, to me, is the soul of the entire production. *The Devil Commands* is not really plot driven; it's character driven. If the movie went over 90 minutes, it would no longer be a B production. So we might have to sacrifice a fine Karloff performance in order to incorporate more plot. Would that be the best choice to make here? *I don't think so!* By allowing the screenwriter to open and explore his can of worms, something more important artistically would be lost.

AJL: The plot I suggested was just to illustrate that I could off the top of my head come up with a more satisfying climax using devices that the screenplay had already set up. Any person with imagination could create a more interesting climax.

It has been too long since I've seen *The Devil Commands* to remember anything in detail except my profound sense of being let down by the screenwriter. If the film went somewhere (anywhere) after its present climax and managed to stay 90 minutes long, we'd still have 90 minutes of Boris Karloff creativity, so I tend to doubt that anything would be lost.

Finally, may I suggest that this discussion is probably the most attention anybody has paid to *The Devil Commands* in decades. If the movie offered more, that would not be the case. Hell, if the movie ended with stock footage from *Dante's Inferno* (1935), we would have been talking about it for years.

GS: So Arthur, you admit you haven't seen *The Devil Commands* in ages! About your charge that the film hasn't received much attention in print in the past decade or so, Michael Price does a chapter on the Columbia Mad Doc series in his revised and definitive *Human Monsters* (Midnight Marquee/Luminary Press, 2004). Don Leifert did an article on them in *Video Review*. And I know I have read several articles on them in magazines within the past 15 years. With all the ink given Monogram, PRC, Universal, and all the rest, the time is ripe to rediscover this quartet of Karloff gems. The debate should be over which entry

Boris Karloff's intensity makes *The Man Who Changed His Mind* work.

is the best: *The Devil Commands, The Man They Could Not Hang, Before I Hang* (1940) or *The Man with Nine Lives* (1940).

But the reason these films have not been discussed in print very often is because of their unavailability on home video. Too many people, like Arthur, remember the film from the dusty past of their memory, not from the definitive home-DVD release. I seem to be forced into the position of over-praising the film... I constantly state it is a B production (which *The Walking Dead* is technically *not*, and of course *Dead* is the superior movie). I happen to enjoy *The Devil Commands* because of two stellar performances, mood, creative photography and an involving plot. To me, a movie should be judged by what it *is* and *not* what each individual wishes it could have been. That is more wish fulfillment than film criticism.

Boris Karloff and Amanda Duff from *The Devil Commands*

The sequence where Karloff's wife is killed is emotionally devastating, and the movie offers big bangs for the buck.

MC: I agree with this whole-heartedly.

GS: I don't see its abrupt ending as a screenwriter cop-out. For me, the film satisfies.

MC: Yes: Overall *The Devil Commands* satisfies. It's a good film! I believe the story ends where it does, as it does, mostly because Dmytryk and company didn't have money to do anything more elaborate.

By the way, Karloff also undergoes a hairdo change in *The Walking Dead*!

GS: I cannot argue and defend all its faults because it is a B production. (I love *The Devil Bat* [1940], but, if I spoke about the film's logic, special effects and hilarious performances—well, I wouldn't love that film as much as I do.) We have to give our beloved Bs some slack, don't we? *The Devil Commands* ("and Karloff obeys," as the merchandising made clear) is not just a film about a scientist who delves into God's domain and gets shut out; it is a film about how far a dedicated scientist and husband will go to keep his dead wife's spirit alive and what depths he will plumb to Not Let Her Go. Thus, it is one of the more romantic-themed horror movies, and the deterioration of Karloff's sanity (symbolized by his radical hairdo change) from the first half to the second half makes this Karloff performance a true gem! It's like Karloff from *Black Friday* (1940) is merged with Janos Rukh from *The Invisible Ray* (1936), all within one movie.

AA: Well, while we were all debating, I *finally* finished watching *The Devil Commands* the other day (loaned to me by the courteous, erudite, and thoughtful Steve Thornton). Here's my thought for a re-edit: If they had started the movie about a half-hour into the picture—at the point where the sheriff comes to the cliff-side manor and questions the housekeeper, they could have extended the story beyond the almost-got-in-touch-with-his-wife-but-then-he-dies ending. With a few further lines of expository dialogue between the housekeeper and the sheriff, everything that came before could have been explained, and the story could have gone on from there. The only thing that *maybe* we would have lost by this approach was the loving relationship depicted between Karloff and his soon-to-be-dead wife in the early scenes (but this could have been remedied by a brief flashback somewhere else in the picture). Then we could have concentrated on the strange relationship between Karloff and the medium (what is the power that she wields over him? what kind of favors [sexual?] does she demand of him for her cooperation?) *and* we could have seen what happens *after* Karloff succeeds in contacting his wife. Since it turns out that his daughter is the *true* medium between him and his wife, what would happen if his wife begins to speak through and possess his daughter? Now, there's a kink worthy of a Lewton movie. Think Columbia could have pulled it off?

AJL: Only if they'd had the will, wit and imagination to try.

GS: But omitting the first third of the movie and creating a new, final third, *The Devil Commands* would not have been the same film, and by sacrificing the film's major focus, the transformation of Karloff's character, plot would have been stressed over characterization, thus destroying the film's major strength. Why not end *Casablanca* by having Bogart and Bergman fly away together or have Bogart's detective play the fool and "take the fall" for the vile Mary Astor villainess at the end of *The Maltese Falcon*? Talk about opening (or not opening) that can of worms!

BLACK FRIDAY
Universal's Horror Fraud
by Nathalie Yafet

Karloff and Lugosi were one of the greatest screen teams in horror film history. In 1939, moviegoers saw them as the Frankenstein monster and his best friend Ygor in the Universal hit *Son of Frankenstein*. In 1940, Universal, hoping that lightning would strike twice, paired the hot team again in *Black Friday*. Eager fans ran to the theater expecting more of their favorite horror duo and instead saw Stanley Ridges and Boris Karloff in the two leads, with Bela Lugosi on the side. Who was Stanley Ridges and what was he doing daring to come between Karloff and Lugosi?

Ridges was a British stage actor who studied under the famous musical comedy star, Beatrice Lillie. He found his way to the States and became a leading man on Broadway, eventually making a splash in the film *Crime Without Passion* that starred a post-*Invisible Man* Claude Rains. Stanley Ridges also appeared in *Sergeant York* and *To Be Or Not to Be*, among others.

Why did Universal decide to switch its leading men? The urban legend, as argued by both Gregory Mank and Tom Weaver, is that Boris Karloff was nervous about the Jekyll/Hyde-inspired Red Cannon/George Kingsley part and instead took Bela Lugosi's role as Eastern European surgeon, Dr. Ernest Sovac. However this whole scenario is based on the words of *Black Friday* screenwriter Curt Siodmak. Siodmak has been quoted, rather extensively (in *Karloff and Lugosi: The Story of a Haunting Collaboration* and in *Universal Horrors*) making sarcastic remarks about Bela Lugosi, such as, "How can a Hungarian be a nice guy" and Lugosi "could never act his way out of a paper bag." It is Siodmak's contention that "Karloff didn't want to play the dual role in *Black Friday*. He was afraid of it... It was too intricate..." The always-humble Karloff may well have expressed negative concerns about playing this dual role. Not that the actor who had successfully pulled off the twin performances of Gregor and Anton (with Gregor impersonating Anton) in *The Black Room* wouldn't have been just fine, but it is more than possible that Siodmak encouraged the cast change, using Karloff's hesitation as an excuse in order to keep Lugosi out of a starring role. It is also difficult to believe that Universal would make changes because they wanted to accommodate an actor's reluctance. After all, this was the same Universal who had reduced Bela Lugosi's $1,000 *Son of Frankenstein* salary to $500 and ordered all his scenes to be wrapped in one week because Hollywood gossip columnist Louella Parsons had leaked the news that the down-on-his-luck

Hungarian actor had applied to The Motion Picture Relief Fund in order to pay the hospital bills for the delivery of his baby boy. Fortunately, director Rowland V. Lee found out and angrily said, "Those God-damned sons of bitches! I'll show them. I'm going to keep Bela on this picture from the first day of shooting right up to the last!" So why wouldn't Universal want to take advantage of "poor Bela" yet again when they had him in their grip on *Black Friday*? Casting Bela Lugosi as Marnay, the gangster, would be a lot cheaper than starring him opposite Karloff as Dr. Ernest Sovac. Acquiring 50-year-old Stanley Ridges (no longer a romantic leading man) for the Kingsley/Cannon role would also suit Universal's economic bottom line.

But *Black Friday* was a fraud from the start. The advertising campaign (the one-sheet poster illustrates the two sinister heads of Karloff and Lugosi in standard horror movie poses) lavished lots of space on images of the horror duo. Fans expected to see not only Karloff and Lugosi but a *horror* film as well. They were cheated on both counts. The two horror kings do not share one single scene in the entire film. Karloff as Kingsley/Cannon and Lugosi as Sovac would have crackled and snapped each time they were on the screen together. Without their magic, *Black Friday*, a noirish gangster movie with a relatively unknown character actor getting most of the screen time, almost fizzles. Is it any wonder that admirers of both actors still discuss the *Black Friday* that might have been?

Boris Karloff as the nattily dressed Dr. Sovac, who fantasizes about building his own laboratory.

Black Friday opens with a calendar rapidly flipping pages until it lands ominously on Friday the 13th (the original title for the film.) Karloff as Sovac is walking that familiar last mile and gives his records to the one newspaper that was fair to him. We eavesdrop as the reporter reads, "I go to my death as a scientist leaving behind this record with the hope that it will benefit mankind..." Think of Bela Lugosi, who had so effectively underplayed the role of Dr. Benet in *The Invisible Ray*, playing Sovac in this scene showing no remorse. Lugosi/Sovac's chief concern would be science as both the end and the means. Next we are treated to an oh-so-cute flashback to Stanley Ridges as Dr. George Kingsley, making bad jokes about a 16th-century poet to his English class on Friday, June 13. Karloff shined performing a similar role in the 1937 Universal film *Night Key*. Audiences always felt sympathy for a Karloff character no matter how heinous the cinematic interpretations were, so just imagine how quickly Karloff's Kingsley would have won audience support as he read poetry and showed real regard for his students.

Professor Kingsley tells his class that he might take another job in a large university, but he is escorted from the classroom by lovely Anne Gwynne playing Jean Sovac, and picked up by dapper Dr. Sovac and Kingsley's wife, Margaret, in order to make a train. Sovac makes a stop so that Kingsley can get his hat. As the professor crosses the street, gunfire is heard, two cars roar into town and Sovac, Margaret and Jean watch in shock while gentle George is thrown violently into a wall by gangster Red Cannon's out-of-control car. Someone in the rival gangster's car shoots Cannon and it speeds away with Bela Lugosi's Eric Marnay stating that "Mr. Red Cannon now belongs to the *history* of crime, past tense." In *Karloff and Lugosi*, Greg Mank says that Lugosi "looks puffy and uncomfortable" like an "old uncle out for a Sunday drive." I see it another way. Lugosi sounds grim, matter-of-fact and he looks dangerous. An ambulance arrives and Sovac accompanies the two injured men. But how much more

Anne Nagel, Stanley Ridges and Bela Lugosi confront one another with tense concern in *Black Friday*.

effective if it had been Lugosi's Dr. Sovac who rides off with Kingsley and Cannon in the back of the ambulance while calmly carrying on a conversation with the severely injured criminal, Cannon. Lugosi had already proven how chilling he could be as the murderously calculating Dr. Orloff in *The Human Monster*, who thinks nothing of polishing off his trusting blind charges in order to collect on their insurance policies.

At the hospital, Sovac illegally transplants the Cannon brain into Kingsley's head in order to save his friend's life. The bizarre operation succeeds and two detectives question Sovac about Cannon. They quip that the gangster "had nothing but the electric chair to live for," a remark which foreshadows Sovac's own end. As Karloff/Sovac unwinds from the strain of murdering one man to save another, he reads in a newspaper about Cannon's $500,000 stash and fantasizes about building his own laboratory with the money. In order to stimulate the Cannon brain into remembering where the cash is hidden, Sovac convinces Kingsley to go with him to New York. This is actually a very effective scene between Karloff and Ridges because Ridges plays his part straight without being maudlin and Karloff's secret agenda is convincingly hidden from his friend, but *not* from us. Effective as it is, the sequence would be more fascinating with Lugosi's nattily dressed Dr. Sovac showing great concern for his professor friend, when all he wants to do is see if the gangster brain remembers where the money is hidden, and Karloff's wretchedly tired and confused Kingsley wondering why he feels so awful.

The men go to New York City, check into Cannon's old hotel haunt and listen to Cannon's girlfriend Sunny sing in a nightclub. The Cannon brain reasserts itself while prompted hypnotically by Sovac. Ridges/Kingsley holds his head in his hands, looks down and becomes Ridges/Cannon while smoothing back his hair. Ridges is suitably mean and tough but the notion that Karloff could not have created an effective dual performance is not consistent with what Karloff did in *The Mummy, The Black Room, The Raven, The Walking Dead* and *Before I Hang*. For example, in *The Black Room* Boris Karloff played twin brothers Anton and Gregor. Bad Gregor murders good Anton by kicking him into a deep pit in the castle's black room and he then impersonates his gracious brother, who had a paralyzed right arm. Gregor observes his reflection in the room's onyx walls and adjusts his expression to resemble Anton's. Karloff makes these moments count by

Fraud from the start? Universal promised horror but here icon Bela Lugosi seems cast more in the gangster mold.

carefully fixing his tousled hair and trying to look respectable while still retaining the mocking evil that is always just waiting to be released. Later, on Gregor/Anton's wedding day, he warns himself, "Never use your right arm again. Never stretch it out..." Here are three Karloff roles and three perfect characterizations.

With the Cannon personality now dominating, Cannon/Kingsley murders one of his traitorous associates, Devore. The killing is done Lewton-style in shadows ending with a close-up of Cannon/Kingsley's evil leering face. Was such a stance a challenge for Boris Karloff? Hardly. Close-ups like these were used in *House of Frankenstein*, *Before I Hang* and all three Karloff/Lewton collaborations. I am just mentioning contemporary 1940s Karloff films here. The list of evil Karloff close-ups is almost as long as his filmography.

Let's return to *Black Friday*. The Jekyll/Hyde gangster is just getting started. Kane, a gang member who tried to get Sunny to talk, is the next one on the vengeful gangster's list. Afterwards, Cannon/Kingsley pays a call on Sunny himself, showing off a fancy watch that Kane had promised her. Another *Black Friday* ongoing argument emerges in this scene. Greg Mank says that (Karloff) "must have had a hard time imagining himself flirting and smooching with Anne Nagle." Tom Weaver says that "it's embarrassing and ridiculous trying to picture a 1940 Karloff... playing kissy-face with Anne Nagel..." He certainly wasn't embarrassing or ridiculous as Dr. Hohner in *The Climax* four years later when telling his lover Marcellina that he "...can't bear the thought that any man can hear you sing for him, feast his eyes on you—just for the price of a ticket." Karloff was all passion in this flashback scene and he was four years older when *The Climax* was made in 1944. Hohner strangles his beloved and then cradles her in his arms, murmuring lovingly, "We'll always be together now..." Nine years later in *Abbott and Costello Meet Dr. Jekyll and Mr. Hyde*, Karloff would have no trouble persuading us that he means business when he ardently tells his young and pretty charge, "You'll not marry anyone but me!" Ten years later in *The Raven*, Karloff as the wily sorcerer Dr. Scarabus has some playfully sexual scenes with Hazel Court who plays Lenore. It is not hard to believe that Lenore and Scarabus do not exactly fill their evenings reading good books. This is all the more incredible given that Boris Karloff was 76 years of age when he appeared

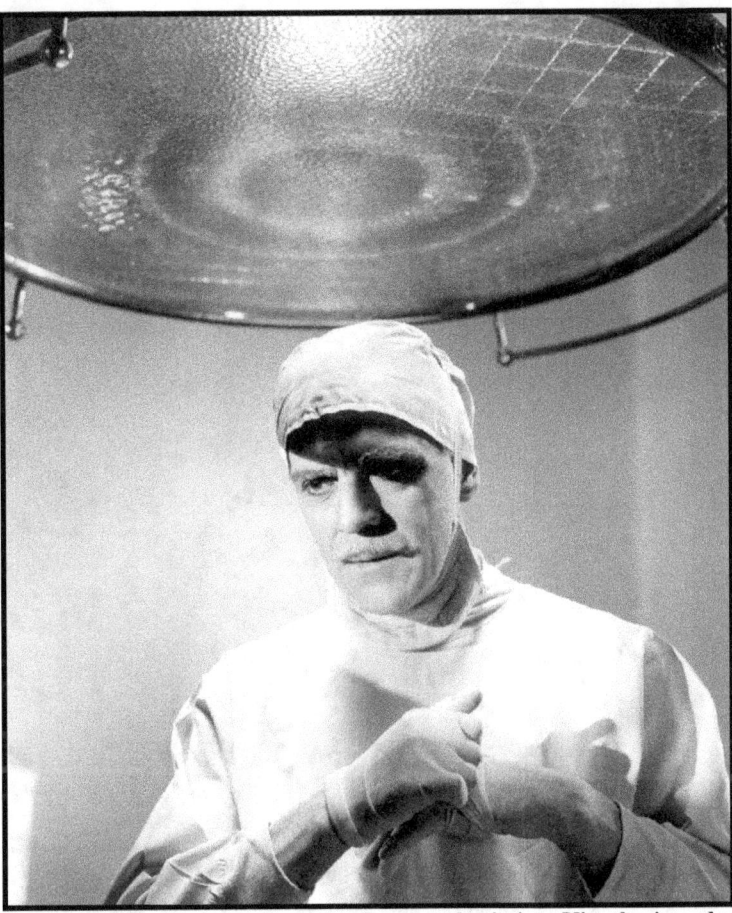

Dr. Sovac illegally transplants the Cannnon brain into Kingsley in order to save his friend's life.

as Scarabus! Given the chance, Karloff was more than up to the challenge. Ironically with so much being made of Ridge's onscreen romantic flair, when Cannon/Kingsley first seeks out Sunny and embraces her, Ridges only manages to mash his face against Anne Nagel's cheek before the suggestive dissolve.

Cannon/Kingsley waits for Lugosi's Marnay at his apartment. Two policemen question him and Cannon/Kingsley kills them with a concealed gun. The remaining policemen chase him over rooftops and down stairs. Time for more *Black Friday* controversy. Tom Weaver calls it "...jumping around urban rooftops." Why has no one ever mentioned the obvious fact that all the athletic long shot fight and chase sequences in this film were done with stunt men? So why is it absurd to think that a different stunt double could have been used for Boris Karloff if he had played the dual George Kingsley/Red Cannon role? Stunt doubles were always used for Karloff in many of his more vigorous films after his back problems started, so why should the action shots on *Black Friday* have been any different?

Cannon/Kingsley, having been wounded in the rooftop chase, goes to Sovac and finds his wife and Sovac's daughter at their hotel. Sovac suavely muscles the

"I go to my death as a scientist," Sovac declares at the beginning of the movie.

ladies out of the room and mistakenly reveals to Cannon/Kingsley that he knows about the loot. The gangster threatens the doctor but is quickly bested when the doctor coldly asks him if he would "...like to be George Kingsley for good..." and commands, "From now on, you'll do exactly as I say." Arguably this is one of the top moments in *Black Friday*, but it could have been better still. Think back to *The Raven* in 1935. The doctor tells his patient to do as he says—or else. Dr. Vollin deliberately paralyzes half of escaped convict Edmund Bateman's face so that the helpless man will have to oblige him with a little "torture and murder." Envision Lugosi's sleek Sovac menacing Karloff's wounded gangster/professor almost snarling as he says, "From now on, you'll do exactly as I say!" This line could have taken a place of honor among other memorable Bela doctor lines such as this gem from *The Raven*, "A doctor is fascinated by death—and pain. And how much pain a man can endure." What a loss for Lugosiphiles!

Dr. Sovac faces off with his daughter, Jean. He is pleased with the outstanding success of the brain transplant even though Cannon is "a gangster and a murderer." She tells him he could go to prison for the illegal operation. Jean wins this one. Sovac will take Kingsley back home.

In the meantime, Sunny tells Cannon/Kingsley that she will go to South America with him after he retrieves the money. But she betrays his confidence immediately to Lugosi's Marnay and another gangster, Miller, who tail Cannon/Kingsley to the reservoir where he has stashed the loot. There's a magnificent, muddy, wet fight as Marnay gets tossed into the reservoir and Miller is killed by Cannon/Kingsley, "brawling in the waterfront dirt..." as described by Tom Weaver in *Universal Horrors*. Great scene, but most of it is once again done with stunt doubles. It is obvious if you watch the sequence several times closely. Even the much praised "brawling in the waterfront dirt..." is not done by Stanley Ridges. Here again, there would have been no trouble getting a stunt double to match Karloff's famous features. While Cannon/Kingsley and Miller are duking it out, Lugosi/Marnay, looking just like a magnificent Warner Bros. cat, sneaks off with the dough. Marnay streaks to Sunny's place where he insinuatingly informs her that now the split on the cash is just between the two of them, but their triumph is brief. Cannon/Kingsley soon shows up and Sunny tells Marnay to hide in the closet. The lying songbird tries to convince the gangster/professor that she hasn't "seen Marnay in six months," but the water and muddy footprints on the floor tell another story. He quickly locks the closet door and shoves the refrigerator in front of it, cutting off Marnay's air supply. The trapped gangster screams out that the money is "in the oven," but the information does not save his life. Marnay suffocates in Sunny's closet while Sunny herself gets snuffed. This is the overly discussed sequence where Bela is really supposed to be hypnotized. What is really the truth here? Lillian Lugosi insists that Bela was not hypnotized. *Black Friday* director, Arthur Lubin, says that it was a publicity stunt. You decide.

After murdering his former sweetheart, Cannon/Kingsley goes back to the hotel with the money where Sovac puts him under hypnosis in order to permanently suppress Red Cannon. Sovac grabs the money and takes Kingsley back home. Not so fast, there is no happy ending. In the classroom, the sound of a police siren reawakens the dormant Cannon and the memory of the metal cashbox. The vicious gangster attacks Jean Sovac demanding his money. Her father hears her screams and shoots his friend. In a Wolf Man-to-Talbot dissolve (Siodmak's homage to himself?), Cannon becomes Kingsley for the final time as he asks Sovac, "Why did you do it? Why, Ernest?" Very touching, indeed, but Karloff was a master at this kind of scene, such as in *The Walking Dead* (a horror picture with gangster overtones) when he played the unjustly condemned John Elman. The poor man knows that he is going to the electric chair for a murder that someone else committed. On his way to death, he looks heavenward with those beautiful eyes and whispers feelingly, "He'll believe me." Perhaps the most famous of these Karloff moments was as the monster in *The Bride of Frankenstein* whose dead eyes overflow with tears when he listens to his new friend the hermit play Schubert's *Ave Maria*.

Other critics besides Tom Weaver have contended that Boris Karloff could not play a plausible gangster. His magnificent Gaffney in Howard Hawks' *Scarface* is proof that he could. The actor sneers, snarls and toughs his way through the brief but pivotal role and his British accent does not lessen the impact that he makes before he is assassinated in a bowling alley. And his suavely romantic nightclub owner, Happy MacDonald, in *Night World* is a gentleman forced to play along with bootleggers and gangsters because of the machinations of his unfaithful wife. Karloff also played grittily realistic criminals in *Graft, Behind the Mask,* and *Dick Tracey Meets Gruesome, The Criminal Code* and *The Miracle Man* getting high marks from reviewers of the day who cited his "naturalistic" style.

Yet another criticism is that Boris Karloff could not handle love scenes. What about his lovesick Imhotep/Ardath Bey in *The Mummy*? Karloff's Dr. Laurience in *The Man Who Changed His Mind* is so gone over his young protégé, Dr. Claire Wyatt, that he is willing to swap bodies with a younger man so that he can have her. There are many compelling scenes in this movie where Dr. Laurience reveals his love for Claire just by locking eyes with her. We do not doubt the strength of this attachment. *The Terror* is certainly not a top-ranking Karloff film, but the Baron Victor von Leppe's speeches about his tenderly remembered dead love resonate. I have

Black Friday **has a noir brain transplanted into a horror body and will always be the great what-if.**

previously mentioned *The Climax, Abbott and Costello Meet Dr. Jekyll and Mr. Hyde* and *The Raven* (1963). Obviously, romance and Karloff were not synonymous in the minds of the studio executives or the public, but he could do it and does it very well indeed.

It is impossible to understand why Universal would tamper with *Black Friday* the way they did after the roaring success of *Son of Frankenstein*, unless we allow for some back lot political maneuvering. Why on earth make a Karloff/Lugosi movie that the studio fully intends to promote as a horror vehicle for the hit team from *The Black Cat, The Raven, The Invisible Ray* and *Son of Frankenstein* when the studio suits dictate they should *never* pass each other in the night? *Black Friday* has a noir brain transplanted into a horror body and will always be regretted as the great what-if. Some things can never be forgotten or forgiven.

Black Friday
CREDITS: Producer: Burt Kelly; Director: Arthur Lubin; Screenplay: Curt Siodmak and Eric Taylor; Photography: Elwood Bredell; Art Director: Jack Otterson; Associate Art Director: Harold MacArthur; Film Editor: Philip Cahn; Musical Director: Hans J. Salter; Gowns: Vera West; Set Decorator: Russell A. Gausman; Sound Supervisor: Bernard B. Brown; Makeup: Jack P. Pierce; Special Effects: John P. Fulton; Technician: Charles Carroll; Running time: 70 minutes; Premiered March 21, 1940; Released: April 12, 1940.

CAST: Boris Karloff (Dr. Ernest Sovac); Bela Lugosi (Eric Marnay); Stanley Ridges (Professor George Kingsley/Red Cannon); Anne Nagel (Sunny Rogers); Anne Gwynne (Jean Sovac); Virginia Brissac (Margaret Kingsley); Edmund MacDonald (Frank Miller); Paul Fix (William Kane); Murray Alper (Bellhop); Jack Mulhall (Bartender); Joe King (Chief of Police); John Kelly (Taxi Driver); James Craig (Reporter); Ellen Lowe (Maid); Jerry Marlowe (Clerk)

BAD MOON RISING: GINGER SNAPS AND DOG SOLDIERS

by Gary J. Svehla

Welcome to the new era of werewolf film! *Ginger Snaps* (2001*)*, the low-budget but slick Canadian film that just happens to be the best werewolf movie produced since Joe Dante's *The Howling* a generation ago. And its sequel *Ginger Snaps 2: Unleashed* (2003), along with *Dog Soldiers* (2002), is a modern werewolf movie worthy of making audiences howl.

Ginger Snaps, written by Karen Walton and directed by John Fawcett, equates a young girl experiencing her first menstrual cycle with lycanthropy (a subtle metaphor for all the unnerving changes in her body, giving special meaning to the phrase "the curse"). At the dinner table one night, quirky, nihilistic Ginger complains of back pains as mother Pamela (a perky and equally odd Mimi Rogers in a superb supporting performance) asks how she hurt her back. Younger sister Brigitte, simply called B, torments her older sister with the impending diagnosis of cancer of the spine, as Pamela is eager that her "three year late" daughter may finally be experiencing womanhood.

But it is the subtle and layered performances that bring to life 16-year-old Ginger (Katharine Isabelle, actually 18) and 15-year-old Brigitte/B (Emily Perkins, actually 22) and makes *Ginger Snaps* a modern horror classic. Perkins and Isabelle make *Ginger Snaps* an anomaly… a character-driven horror movie that relegates the werewolf to only two sequences. The girls and their antics carry the entire movie, aided in large part by pithy, intelligent dialogue that keeps these teens and their uncertainty and pain rooted in reality.

For their school project the girls enact a series of photos/slides of the sisters dying horrible deaths. As Ginger gleefully declares, "Our deaths will *rock*." B answers, "You don't think our death should be *more* than *cheap* entertainment?" By movie's end the viewer will come to realize these individual quotes define the personality of each girl. Right from the start we learn that Ginger is a poseur, a drama queen, who romanticizes the concept of death, while odd-duck B cherishes life. These eccentric sisters are obsessed with their death pact to always be together. Ginger reminds B, "Suicide is the ultimate fuck you. Come on, it's so *us*. It's the pact!" B, referred to as "the dweeb" by a group of high school boys, tells Ginger, "the redhead with the rack," "It's so easy for you… you don't care." To which Ginger smiles and declares: "Dead by 16… out of the scene… together forever." The two girls lock their flat palms together, revealing slash marks on both their hands.

Their school slide project is revealed one day in class. One sister, face up, is impaled on a white picket fence, her eyes wide open; another shot shows a sister curled up underwater in the bathtub; another shows a sister crushed under the wheels of a car, blood oozing from her mouth; another shows a girl lying dead on the grass, a lawnmower on top of her, a cigarette still burning in her mouth; etc. In this manner the sisters gleefully celebrate their flipping-finger attitude and outcast status.

The required werewolf attack, shot in a park playground at night, comes as the sisters are planning to kill classmate Trina's dog and make it seem as though the beast that has slaughtered pets in the community has struck again. Blood begins to drip down Ginger's thigh as the girls find the devoured remains of a dog in the park. "B, I just got the curse," Ginger reveals in disgust. "You kill yourself to be different, but your body screws you. If I start hanging around tampon dispensers or start talking about PMS, just shoot me." Eerily, the hobbyhorse nearby slightly sways and all grows quiet as Ginger is suddenly attacked and dragged screaming through the nearby woods. B, her breathing heavy and labored, frantically searches calling out her sister's name, but all she hears are screams in the distance. We can hardly see the beast that is attacking, only quick flashes of snout and teeth and fur. Finally B, armed with a branch, beats the beast off Ginger, and both girls run toward the road and safety, where the werewolf is splattered by a van driven by greenhouse keeper and likable drug dealer Sam (Kris Lemche). No Hollywood mythology (silver bullets) is at work here. In a marvelous follow-up sequence, B gets Ginger home, screaming in pain and covered in blood, huge claw marks running down her shoulder and chest. But within a minute Ginger declares she's not bleeding anymore and her wounds are already healing.

While Ginger's transformation to werewolf is slow, her transformation from outcast to sex queen is sudden, as she soon finds herself playfully attacking boys on the athletic field and smoking pot in the back of vans. However, Ginger is unnerved when she invites B into the school bathroom stall to show her tufts of hair growing out of her slash wounds. "I can't have a hairy chest, B, that's fucked!" Soon Ginger will also sprout a phallic tail.

But Ginger and B start to move further apart. Ginger becomes paranoid thinking B is jealous of her expanding social/sexual cycle, but in reality B is simply worried about her sister's unnatural physical and personality changes. Ginger accuses B of being the monster with little green eyes, to which B answers in her totally honest way: "Yes, I always wanted to hemorrhage and be hairy and suck off Jason McCarthy" (the popular boy with whom she is getting *busy*)! Later that night Ginger is in a car with Jason and she makes all the aggressive sexual moves. Jason, obviously not comfortable being used as a sex toy, cries, violet, her long, straight hair covering her face, her eyes darting downward when speaking, always reluctant to make eye contact. Sam comes up with a potential cure Aconitum, or monkshood, a naturally growing poison (with blue flowers) that Sam describes as a natural detox that promotes the growth of red blood cells, similar to wolfbane.

But as Ginger transforms into a sexually active teen, she also grows jealous of B's attraction to Sam. When teen bitch Trina confronts B outside their yard and demands the return of her dog, the bestial Ginger grabs Trina from behind, playfully taunting and slapping her on her forehead. Ginger utters: "You play with your new friends, I'll play with mine… You asked for this, you picked Sam over me. Whatever happens now, it's your fault!" The fight escalates into the Fitzgerald kitchen and milk is spilled on the floor, and when Trina grabs a knife she slips, impaling herself, her blood blending with the puddles of milk as she crumples in death. Hiding the body in the freezer, the girls quickly stage one of their death photo shoots making out the real blood is only for show as their parents rush into the kitchen. Mother Pamela utters: "I told you, *no* more deaths in the house!"

After digging the corpse out of the family freezer with an ice pick, Ginger longingly looks at the blood-matted corpse of Miss Popularity and asks B seriously, "Do you think she is pretty?" B just as seriously asks, "If I wasn't here, would you *eat* her?" Ginger, in disgust, mutters, "No! God! That would be like *fucking* her." Once again Ginger's confused violent/sexual urges baffle her. But these lines of dialogue demonstrate Ginger's inability to cope with all the changes her body is undergoing. Later Ginger playfully kills the janitor at school, ultimately digging her fingernails into his stomach: "I didn't like the way he looked at you, B!" Then Ginger continues, describing her urges: "I like it, it feels so… good. It's like touching yourself. Every move, right on the fucking dot, and after… fucking fireworks, supernovas, a goddamn force of nature!" As B crawls away fearfully from Ginger,

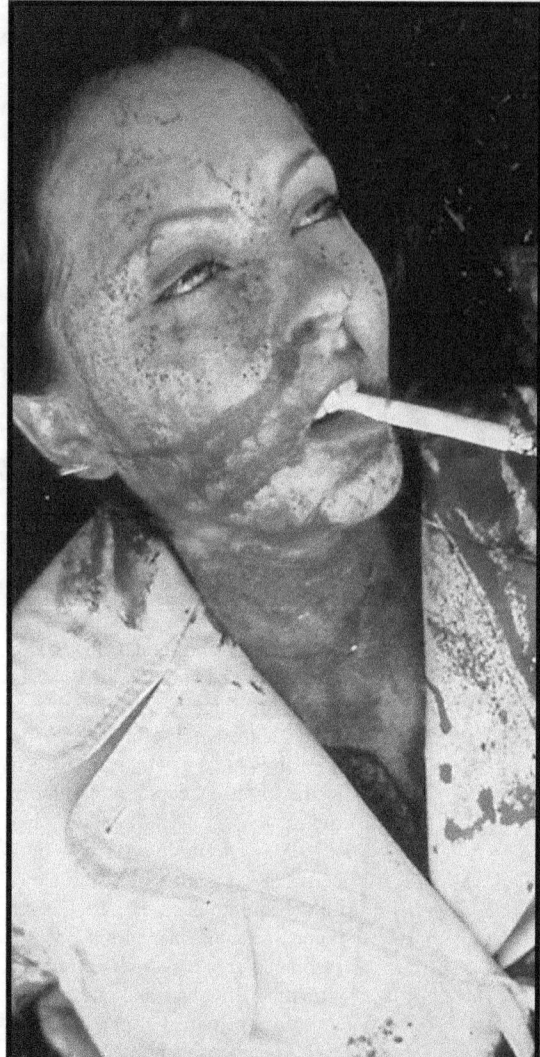

Katharine Isabelle as Ginger from *Ginger Snaps*

"Take it easy, we got all night." Ginger tells him to lay back and relax, as she tears his shirt off. Jason's last frantic words are "who's the boy here!!!" as Ginger's rough sex commences.

Yet Ginger is not as strong or as independent as she pretends, as she runs home to her sister and vomits blood in the toilet. Fearfully, Ginger admits, "Something is very wrong. I had this urge… I thought it was for sex, but it was to tear every fucking thing to pieces!!!" Admitting to herself that Jason's "the hero" and that I'm just "the freak, mutant lay," Ginger admits she killed the neighbor's dog to satisfy her urge, that she couldn't help herself, and that she feels "wicked," flashing her new wolfish teeth.

B is forced to enlist Sam, the guy with the green thumb and interest in chemistry and, surprisingly, B. B is the shrinking

The werewolf model used in *Ginger Snaps*

Ginger, very feline, hovers menacingly over B. Ginger almost purrs, "You would love it, a little scratch, swap some juice… it would be our own pact, just like before, it's so *us* B!" But B tells her, "I'd rather be dead than be what you are!" But Ginger reminds her, "We have a pact! Dead by 16!" When B refuses, Ginger tells her sister to stay out of her way.

That evening Ginger makes her grand entrance at the party at the greenhouse. Ginger's looks have changed as her hair is now blonde, her eyes appear animal-like, the structure of her face less human, her exposed stomach leathery. But she is now a smoldering creature of sensuality and immediately makes a play to seduce the *unwilling* Sam, to win her sister back by proving Sam to be only a sex-obsessed creep (such is not the case). But since the medicine is back at their home, B has to get Ginger there, and the only way is for her to finish the new blood pact, cutting her hand, cutting Ginger's, and joining palms together (thus infecting B with the virus) to again win her sister's trust. "You got everything from me that isn't about you… now I *am* you," B bellows. To which frightened Ginger responds, "But what am I?"

By the movie's climax Ginger is no longer human. In the back of Sam's van, her body contorts and she spits up blood as her human shell becomes twisted and shed. Ginger finally loses the last vestiges of her humanity as she becomes the werewolf. The pulse-pounding finale features a slow trek through the darkened family home, Sam and B armed only with a flashlight and syringe of monkshood. Sam volunteers to administrator the drug. But once out of the kitchen, Sam is brutally attacked, banged against furniture and dragged down to the cellar. B, gasping for breath, slowly leaves the kitchen and finds the still-intact syringe, which she clutches as she heads downward to find her sister. Downstairs B follows the puddles of blood until she hears Sam, who lies broken, beaten and near death on the floor. The werewolf hovers right over him as he sits bleeding, gasping, unconscious. B attempts to suck the blood from her fingers, but she vomits it all up crying, "I can't, I won't." The wolf grows more violent while Sam's body slumps over, apparently dead. B manages to fetch

Together forever! Ginger and B (Emily Perkins) declare "dead by 16" from *Ginger Snaps*.

a knife from the drawer as the werewolf approaches her. "Come on, it's me…Ginger, please, it's me!" Then the determined B declares, "I'm not dying in this room with you… I'm not dying!" Philosophically B is declaring the fundamental difference that always existed between Ginger and her. As the werewolf approaches, its snout inches away from B's face, the animal suddenly slumps over, the knife now buried deep in the beast's torso. Tears well up in B's eyes as she scans her shared bedroom and sees the photos of her sister. B's face is bloodied and pained, the needle still held unused in her hand. The werewolf breathes slowly and B hugs the fiend that was her sister, even after its labored breathing ceases. The camera pans back to show the two sisters' beds in the background.

Ginger Snaps 2, like most sequels, is inferior to the original, but it still has merit. Brett Sullivan replaces original director John Fawcett (back only as executive producer) and Megan Martin becomes the new screenwriter.

Ginger Snaps 2 is primarily flawed because Ginger (Katharine Isabelle) died at the end of the first movie, so the marvelous angst-driven interaction between actresses Emily Perkins

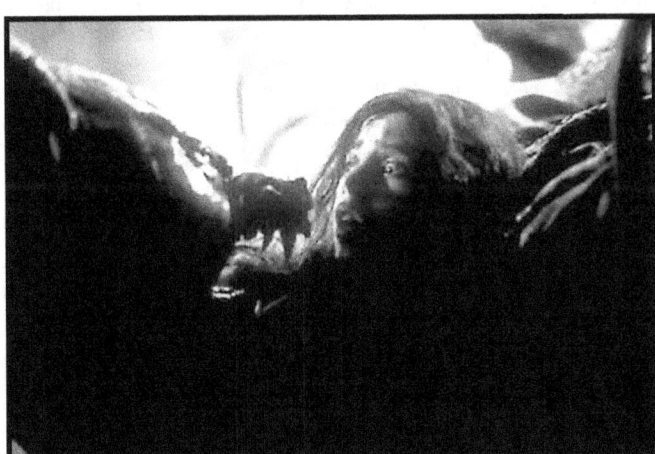

B confronts her sister Ginger, now a wolf, from *Ginger Snaps*.

Emily Perkins makes the older and now wiser sister B the centerpiece of *Ginger Snaps 2*.

and Isabelle is woefully missing. The screenplay does occasionally introduce Isabelle as the ghostly conscience to B, but her screen time is minimal. Perkins has to carry the creative bulk of the movie, but she now has the eccentric character of Ghost (Tatiana Maslany) as her foil. Maslany offers an intense performance, but it is one that is larger than life and lacks the "keeping it real" quality that Katharine Isabelle created.

Ginger Snaps 2 opens with B mainlining monkshood and using knives to cut the bestial flesh from her body. She methodically records the healing time in her journal. Unlike Ginger, B understands the full progression of the disease and she approaches her predicament scientifically. Sister Ginger's ghostly presence appears: "You're healing faster… that doesn't stop it, nothing will stop it… what are you doing, you already dosed today!" B's body goes into seizure. Ginger climbs into bed beside her, but once the camera angle changes, the audience sees no one is on the bed with her, that Ginger's presence is only in B's mind. Ginger, the sister who chose death over life, becomes B's Freudian id encouraging B to give in to her bestial impulses, to accept the fact that she is now a werewolf and no longer human. During this monkshood reaction moment, a young librarian comes to B's apartment to deliver a book on bloodletting, but thinking she has overdosed, he carries her down to his car to get help. Soon a werewolf attacks and tears the young man apart. B awakens lying in a hospital bed, an IV attached to her hand, groggy and weak. She's been admitted to a community outreach center, apparently considered to be just another youthful addict who overdosed.

B takes injections of monkshood to prevent her transformation into beast, but at the center she is monitored 24-7 with plenty of counseling to occupy her time. Alice, her counselor, prides herself in knowing every current drug used/abused. But monkshood is quite another story. "I didn't recognize it myself." To which B counters with her blunt: "Must be great to be a role model." B ends up locked in her room after threatening Alice with: "If you keep me here, people are going to die!" Once more clever, intelligent dialogue bubbles forth, once again becoming the film's major strength. B also takes part in group therapy with a black counselor Eleanor whose smile is plastic and transparent. "Brigitte, you have a roomful of people pretty curious in Brigitte." B stares the perpetually smiling counselor down and utters in rapid-fire spurts: "My best-case scenario, Eleanor, is hair everywhere *but* my eyeballs, elongation of my spine until my skin splits, teeth, and maybe even a growing tolerance for… maybe even an affection for, the taste of feces, not just my own, and then *excruciating* death." By now Eleanor's smile has become a dazed expression of shock as she scribbles in her book, "Brigitte… lesbian?" and underlines *lesbian*.

Because of lack of funding, this hospital is a dual care facility, housing both people with a chemical dependency and also chronic care patients. Enter Ghost, a teenager who sneaks comics from her hidden cubby-hole and watches over her grandmother Barbara, a severely burned woman, whose entire body is wrapped in gauze (her wide and frantic eyes, darting from side to side, appear to be *screaming*). As B is led down the hallway, IV in her arm, Ghost flitters by babbling in her usual over-dramatic way. Ghost often refers to people in the third person, most likely because she is scripting her own graphic novel of the events at hand, merging real life with fiction. Interestingly, her horror comics deal with werewolves as mythical creatures who can only be killed with a silver bullet, but in the world of *Ginger Snaps 2*, lycanthropy is not mythic at

Tatiana Maslany as Ghost becomes the new foil to B, but her performance becomes larger than life.

all, it is simply a blood-borne pathogen. Ghost constantly hangs around B and the two become friendly, if not quite friends.

Meanwhile Ginger once again becomes jealous of B's "cool new friends." B, without monkshood, tells her sister "it's starting." And the only hope Ginger can offer is: "Well, you have two options… either give in or give up. It only dies if you do." Even in death, Ginger feels bonded to her sister and reacts with jealousy whenever B gets close to another human being. It is obvious that Ginger feels only death will bring the sisters together.

In the pivotal sequence of the film, Ghost and B go exploring in the institute's cellar hoping to find an exit in the still-intact crematorium. There, the girls spy Tyler, a male nurse, as he receives oral sex from hottie Beth-Ann who is rewarded with a noseful of cocaine. In her coked up condition she mutters: "I just saw the freakiest thing… it was like an animal but it was deformed…" Immediately B's eyes register panic as she whips around to see something attack Beth-Ann, the predator pressing her horrified face against plastic sheets, which insulate wooden framing. The wolf snorts and Beth-Ann screams as blood spurts and the plastic turns red. One more scream and then silence. Blood saturates the floor and B sees the body of the werewolf disappear around a corner. Soon the growling grows closer as the two girls scream and run for cover as frantic tracking shots, low to the ground, pursue them (some tracking shots are ahead of them looking back, while others become the subjective shots of the wolf, looking ahead, closing the gap). The duo makes its way to the crematorium, but the wolf bites into B's leg, pulling her back, forcing her head against the cold stone wall, shattering tiles upon impact. Immediately sitting up, B straightens her obviously broken leg and pulls a shard out of her chest (reminding the viewer than B is not longer quite human). In the next sequence, B lies flat on her stomach, her eyes wide open in fear, as the werewolf sniffs her upper body. B gasps for breath but remains motionless. Ghost creates a diversion by kicking a can, drawing the wolf away, as B gets up and runs. The girls are able to escape. B tells Ghost that the wolf wanted to mate with her… "Don't try too hard to visualize that!"

During the film's final third, Ghost and B take shelter at Barbara's house where Ghost at first tells a twisted tale that Barbara was set on fire by being caught in a string of malfunctioning Christmas tree lights. Ghost's inappropriate laughter interrupts… "I was just shitting you," and she instead tells B that Barbara was simply smoking in bed. Later when Tyler enters the scene, Ghost implies, in a disheveled state, that Tyler assaulted her. B gains revenge by trapping Tyler outside the garage where the werewolf brutally attacks him. Ghost's character, living isolated in a hospital filled with disturbed addicts, sees B as both the sister and family she craves. Ghost constantly speaks of "sleepovers" and other girlie things once they occupy Barbara's former home. Tatiana Maslany's performance is creepy, menacing and overtly theatrical. Emily Perkins creates a true human transforming into a wolf, while Maslany's performance is never grounded in reality.

Despite injections of monkshood, B is rapidly changing. In a wonderful sequence, Ghost surprises B while she is brushing her now wolfish teeth, the foam making her appear rabid, the brushing so fierce that her bleeding gums cake her teeth with blood. The startled B growls and she seems animalistic, ready to strike. "It's just me!!" Ghost cries out in fear, as B regains her composure.

Captain Ryan turns into a werewolf in *Dog Soldiers*.

After Tyler's death Ginger returns: "You can't fight what's in us B!" B responds, "I'm not like you Ginger, I'm stronger!" Ginger, smiling, states, "That's not how I remember you the first 15 years of your life." And B, always the clever one, responds, "That's how I remember you the last 15 minutes of yours!" Sibling rivalry extends from beyond the grave. Ginger opts for death while B struggles for life as a human being.

By the film's now predictable ending, B finally figures out that Barbara never smoked and Ghost purposely set her on fire. Then B realizes Tyler never raped Ghost, that Ghost concocted the story because "he was going to take you away from me." Alice is killed by Ghost with a sudden hammer blow to the forehead and B, becoming more wolfish by the hour, pleads for Ghost to "kill me" with her cocked rifle. But the demented bad seed only shoves B back down into the cellar and locks the trap door to contain her.

Ginger Snaps 2 shines most brightly during the movie's first half where the story focuses on B and her desperate attempt to remain human. The film's second half goes astray when it focuses more on Ghost and her demon child predictability. The ending is cleverly offbeat, but B's relegation to a purgatory state is unsatisfying. The third and final entry of the *Ginger Snaps* series was released after this article was finished.

Dog Soldiers, a Grand Duchy of Luxembourg/U.K. co-production, transports the modern werewolf film from the world of dysfunctional teens living in quiet suburbia to the action/adventure frontier of military maneuvers in rural Scotland. Writer, editor, director Neil Marshall creates a cleverly crafted exercise in horror bookended with events occurring at the very beginning that have importance at the very end.

The pre-credits sequence shows a middle-aged couple camping in the wilds of Scotland, she giving him a solid silver letter opener as a present. "It's perfect," he states. The couple is next cuddled up inside their tent, preparing for lovemaking, as he gently unzips her pants. However, simultaneously, the tent zipper is also pulled down revealing a quick flash of a beast that whips the man around the tent. She is slowly pulled out of the tent, dragged by her feet. In fear, he looks on and reaches for his sharp letter opener, his eyes rising to meet the fiend, who is growling and howling.

After the credits, now in North Wales, we focus on Private Cooper and Captain Ryan during military maneuvers. Cooper fights and punches until Ryan, armed with a massive dog, points a pistol at Cooper's temple. "Nice try Cooper! You evaded capture for 22 hours and 47 minutes. Go straight to the head of the class!" Ryan helps Cooper to his feet. Things go sour when Ryan hands Cooper his pistol and tells him to shoot the dog. Cooper refuses. Ryan reminds him "that's a direct order!" Cooper screams defiantly, "No, sir!" Ryan bellows,

A moody shot of a werewolf stalking humans in *Dog Soldiers*.

"How can you be on my team if you can't even kill a dog!" Cooper explains, "I didn't say I couldn't kill a dog, sir. I simply said I wouldn't kill that dog for no reason!" Ryan responds bluntly, "I don't need a man with a conscience," and he shoots the dog to Cooper's outrage. Ryan tells his men to send Cooper back to his own squad.

Four weeks later, Cooper is embarking upon training maneuvers with his squad consisting of Sergeant Wells, Bruce, Spoon, Joe, Terry, etc. Most of the men wear close-cropped hair, look similar, and become one large ensemble with Sarge and Cooper standing out as individuals. Within a brief time, the audience feels we know these men intimately. First of all, Wells' rag-tag squad of grunts is up against Special Ops (headed by Captain Ryan) on an "exercise" that is "hardly life or death." A few of the men complain they will miss seeing one of the most important soccer games of the season "without a six pack or a telly." The Sarge states "what I want to do is get home, jump into a warm bath with a nice hot woman and watch the footy." However he reminds his men "we are 50 k. behind enemy lines and if we make contact I want nothing less than gratuitous violence from the lot of you!" Such dialogue humanizes the soldiers.

Soldiers with automatic weapons vs. werewolves, from *Dog Soldiers*

Then, in the best tradition of the campfire story, Cooper shares his story of Eddie Oswald. It was 1991 and Eddie had a tattoo put on his ass to commemorate the occasion. Eddie felt "his soul belonged to God but his flesh was way beyond redemption." Soon Eddie triggered an anti-tank mine and was blown to bits. "It really puts things into perspective when you have to scoop your mate up with a shovel and put him into a bag." Everything was burned to a crisp, except a piece of Eddie with the tattoo. So you can say that Eddie was right, "Satan did indeed save his skin, but just not *all* of it! Or you can say that Eddie was just unlucky. Anyway, it taught me to keep an open mind!" This little story demonstrates the camaraderie of the platoon, as well as demonstrating the infinite struggle between God and Satan, between good and evil. It also demonstrates how fate plays cruel tricks and that keeping an open mind matters.

Keeping an open mind remains the order of the day as Wells' squad comes upon the Special Ops squad slaughtered, no bodies, just blood. "They never got a round off!" The only survivor is Captain Ryan himself who is wounded. Ryan starts ranting, "There was only supposed to be one! You have to get me out of here before they come back…" The Sarge tells Ryan to shut up, "You are scaring my lads." The squad moves out in strict military formation fully armed and ready for attack. The trees gently sway and in the distance an animal's howl can be heard. A quick shadow passes across the sight line of one soldier. However, his rifle jams, the soldier soon abandoning it as he makes a run for safety. The Sarge comes to his rescue too late, and the Sarge has his stomach slashed by one of the werewolves. Soon Cooper saves his superior's life as he enters blasting, scaring the animals off momentarily. Cooper literally shoves the Sarge's guts back into his body as we cut to quick shots of the wolves darting between trees standing on two legs. Soon a woman in a Jeep pulls up and the men immediately jump in, the woman taking them to the nearest home, an isolated one out in the thick of the woods, shrouded in fog. No one appears to be home, but there's a fire burning in the fireplace and plenty of food to be consumed. Soon a beast tries to push in the front door, as the household dog begins to pull at one of Sarge's protruding intestines. But automatic fire scares the beast off. Meanwhile, Ryan is ready to shoot the dog again, but one of the soldiers vomits all over the back of Ryan's head, distracting him and saving the pet.

Megan, a zoologist, states their enemy "is smart… working as a team, looking for a weakness, a way in." When Cooper asks what we are dealing with here, she bluntly answers: "Not entirely wolf, not human, something in between." Suddenly a shadow of a wolf appears outside, and Cooper orders only short, controlled bursts to be fired, to preserve their ammo. Megan and Cooper use Krazy Glue to repair Sarge's intestines.

When the wolves ultimately attack, it is a gripping sequence packed with quick editing, effective lighting and balls-out horror. The door shakes, the window is shattered and a wolf appears. Another wolf crashes through another

In *Dog Soldiers* soldiers face werewolves in hand-to-hand combat.

window. Short bursts of automatic weapons fire greet the onslaught, as the animals growl and grunt. Quick cuts back and forth show the wolves fleetingly, with sound effects rather than visuals creating the tension. A boiling pot of steaming water is thrown on one wolf's head as it pokes through the broken glass in the door. Another wolf reaches through the boarded up slats of a window, grabbing a solder from behind. Cooper comes in armed with a sword and cuts off the wolf's arm. Upstairs, the full lumbering form of an upright wolf climbs through the window in the bedroom where Sarge is sleeping. Cooper enters and dives under the bed, desperately trying to reach his weapon while furiously screaming, "Sarge, wake up!!!" The Sarge awakens, fires his weapon, allowing Cooper time to get his as well. Now several wolves are perched outside windows, but the automatic weapon firing drives them back. Morning has arrived, all is quiet, and the soldiers have survived the attack. We see the house bathed in sunlight. One soldier stands alone, his back to the boarded up window. Confidently, he mutters, "Dogs… more like pussies!" Suddenly, a werewolf breaks through the boards, grabs the soldier and pulls him screaming outside. Terry is gone. Megan offers more doom and gloom. "Before today you felt there was a fine line between myth and reality. Those things out there are real. If they are real, what else is real? You know what's in the shadows now. You might never get another night's sleep as long as you live."

Megan reveals a beat up old Jeep lies in the barn, so the men use one soldier to act as decoy, as another soldier attempts to hot-wire the vehicle to get the survivors out of harm's way. To his horror, the soldier in the Jeep sees before him a wolf slowly tightening its claws around the bloodied head of Terry, his arms outstretched as though begging for help. But the wolf bites down on his neck and head, literally popping it like a balloon, spraying his blood all over the front windshield of the vehicle. The victim's decapitated head sits in a bloody puddle near the Jeep. The soldier in the jeep sits, stares straight ahead… we hear the breathing of a wolf. The man glumly states, "You're behind me, aren't you?!!!" Turning rapidly around, the brave soldier engages the werewolf in hand-to-hand combat, the vehicle rocking and increasingly splattered in blood. The humans inside rush to the barn to find the one soldier slumped over dead and the werewolf in the back seat. They open fire on the beast.

Back at the house Ryan finally reveals the truth. "Ever heard of Special Weapons Division? They're the men in white coats who train dolphins to place mines on submarines and teach furry animals to tear your head off at the neck." Ryan's job was to capture a living werewolf and bring it back for study, but his squad underestimated the number of beasts. Ryan admits, "You were my bait." However, as Ryan gets more emotional, he hisses and displays sharp teeth. He slumps behind a table, and when emerging, his head darts around and his eyes turn animalistic and yellow, his werewolf teeth now revealed. In pain Ryan again slumps behind the table, as we watch his human fingers turn to claws with long, sharp nails. The full wolf now emerges as soldiers are hurled across the room. The werewolf Ryan jumps through a window to escape. Cooper, looking at a Celtic family portrait, states, "Werewolves spend most of their time in human form… they are home." Making an analogy to *Goldilocks and the Three Bears*, Cooper states: "We slept in their fucking beds, eat their porridge… no wonder they are pissed off." For a split second the audience imagines the soldiers are interlopers with the wolves simply protecting their homes. In one last ditch effort, Cooper uses the vehicle in the barn to attempt to lure the wolves there, and then, he ignites the car, escaping, before the barn blows up and burns.

However, Megan reveals the truth upon his return. "I came to be at one with nature, well, I got what I wanted." At this moment Cooper figures out that Megan does not live in a neighboring house in the glen as she claimed, that no wolves were in the barn when it exploded. Cooper comes to understand at last: "You women, the same old shit!" Megan responds, "Being nice to women will get you nowhere Cooper; being nice to me will get you killed! You might think they're all bitches, but I'm the real thing. Do you think I like being part of this fucked up family? Do you think I chose to run with the pack? All we can do is let nature take its course." In a sense this movie becomes the ultimate battle of the sexes with the macho military—all male—battling the female nester. Also, the concept of dysfunctional family achieves a new perversity as a human family becomes a pack of wolves. Megan continues: "They were always here… I simply unlocked the door, it's that time of month." Once again menstrual blood attracts the predatory beast. Slowly, wolves appear behind Megan as her eyes turn yellow and she opens her foul-looking mouth, fangs bared. Cooper shoots her point blank in the head, but now the wolves, inside the house, defend their home against human intruders.

Humans fight valiantly, heroically, but they are doomed to die. The Sarge, at first holding a werewolf off with a lighted aerosol can, resorts to using kitchen pots and pans to bash in the wolf's skull, to no avail. The wolf finally holds Sarge with one claw, its head moving eerily closer, slowly, for the kill. "I hope I give you the shits, you fucking wimp," and he spits in the wolf's face as Sam the dog watches quietly. One soldier manages to attract several of the wolves before blowing the house sky high by igniting a gas line. But finally it is Ryan and Cooper locking horns in the last battle to the death. "Licking your own balls yet?" Cooper asks as the wolf whips him around. "I forgot… you don't have any!" Finally, Cooper

fortuitously finds the solid silver letter opener (the wife's gift from the opening sequence) and stabs the wolf in the neck. He then reaches for his pistol, firing multiple times point blank, saturating the screen with wolf's blood. In the morning, Cooper emerges from the still smoldering ruins of the house, now traveling with Sam the dog alongside. Ironically, the man who hated animals became one himself, and even his bestial transformation cannot provide the edge that Ryan needed. The animal lover Cooper, who befriends Sam the dog, survives the rampage of the beasts because in part he is able to differentiate domestic pet from predatory ravager. To Cooper not all animals are alike. Cooper's humanity and subtle ability to distinguish gives him the winning edge and he survives. During the end credits, Cooper's photo graces the cover of the British tabloid *Express Mail* with the headline: "Werewolves Ate My Platoon!"

How many more times can we watch our Universal Legacy box set version of *The Wolf Man* or *Werewolf of London*? These three modern movies add bite and originality to the werewolf genre, making us once again fearful of the full moon and demonstrating that quality monster movies actually exist on DVD in the modern era.

• MIDNIGHT MARQUEE PRESS, INC. •
• WE KNOW MOVIES! •

Italian Horror
by Jim Harper
$25.00
Discover a whole new world of horror as Harper introduces readers to Italy's film frightfests.

Spawn of Skull Island
THE MAKING OF KING KONG
Turner & Price
$40.00 (hardcover)
Get ready for the Jackson remake by reading this loving history of the original!

Boris Karloff: A Gentleman's Life
by Scott Nollen
Highly praised bio of the legendary Karloff!
$25.00

• • • •

Peter Cushing: An Autobiography and Past Forgetting
by Peter Cushing
We are pleased to offer this reprint with a new chapter by Joyce Broughton.
$25.00

• • • •

Carnival of Souls Graphic Novel
by Michael Price
96 page
GN of the cult film
$12.00

• • • •

Minds of Fear
by Calum Waddell
Interviews with dozens of modern horror film masters including David Cronenberg.
$25.00

• • • •

The Eurospy Guide
by Matt Blake and David Deal
One of our most popular books introduces fans to European spy thrillers from the '60s.
$25.00

• • • •

MidMar Actors Series Vincent Price
MidMar writers contribute chapters on favorite Price films.
$25.00

• • • •

A Gallery of Stars: The Story of the Hollywood Brown Derby's Wall of Fame
by Jack Lane
$25.00
Lane looks at the Golden Age of Hollywood alongside his many caricatures that hung in the Derby and are beautifully reproduced in this book.

• • • •

Some friends and I recently attended a screening of *Jaws* at the Arclight Theaters in Los Angeles. The event was part of the theater's "Storytellers" series and featured appearances by writer Carl Gottlieb and cinematographer Bill Butler, who spoke about the film after the screening. It was great to hear these old pros talking about what went into the production and how much of the success of the film came from problems they faced during its making. *Jaws* has always been a favorite of mine and my friends so we were naturally excited to see the picture again. To further whet our appetites, we watched the *E! True Hollywood Story: Jaws* again (I had, of course, recorded it). But after viewing that program and listening to the guest speakers, I realized something. Everyone talks about the influences on *Jaws* and mentions Ibsen's *Enemy of the People*, *Moby Dick*, *Creature from the Black Lagoon* and even Alfred Hitchcock. But no one has ever mentioned what I'm sure *had* to be a major influence on the film. I'm talking about the 1957 science fiction classic *The Monster That Challenged the World* which is, not coincidentally, my favorite "giant bug" movie from the 1950s and, except possibly for *The Thing*, my favorite 1950s sci-fi flick, period.

Watching *The Monster That Challenged the World* once more, I was able to find at least six or seven instances in plot, theme or character that have similar reflections in *Jaws*. It still surprises me that no one ever picked up on them (as far as I know). In the pages to come, I will analyze *The Monster That Challenged the World* and point out the moments that *Jaws* seems to be referencing. Then the reader can decide for him- or herself whether they are coincidences or scholarly omission. I will also re-evaluate the film to show why it should be regarded as one of the classics of 1950s science fiction.

The Monster That Challenged the World takes place at a naval research base on Southern California's Salton Sea. The scientists there are engaged in atomic experiments while the military conducts daily parachute tests. But, unknown to both parties, an earthquake has opened up a deep fissure under the sea. A parachutist disappears after a routine jump and, soon after, the two sailors looking for him (one of them played by Beach Party regular Jody McCrea) are attacked by something from beneath the depths.

Commander "Iron Heart" Twillinger (Tim Holt), the base's new investigative officer, immediately looks into the matter. Having only been onsite for a week, Twillinger has already earned a reputation among the men as a "tough nut." Twillinger and his rescue party find the abandoned boat covered with a strange goopy liquid. They also find the dead body of one of the sailors, later revealed to have been frightened to death. As the men take a sample of

the mysterious goop, the paratrooper's body surfaces. In a great shock moment, the chutist's head comes into view—shriveled and distorted. This is *Jaws* reference #1—officials investigate an abandoned boat and are frightened by a dead body's ravaged face—just like Brody and Hooper when they find Ben Gardner's boat… followed soon after by Hooper getting scared by Gardner's ravaged corpse underwater. Both sequences stand as uniquely shocking moments.

No-nonsense Twillinger immediately launches a full-scale investigation. While visiting Dr. Rogers (Hans Conreid) at the lab, Twillinger is upset by the fact that Rogers' secretary Gail (Audrey Dalton) has already heard about the accident. Twillinger suspects that the water in the sea has become radioactive but Rogers assures him that the lab's experiments have nothing to do with the deaths of the soldiers. While Twillinger waits for results, he annoyingly listens to Gail banter with Connie Blake (Marjorie Stapp), the pregnant wife of Rogers' assistant George (Dennis McCarthy). But he soon reveals a tender side when he plays with Gail's daughter Sandy (Mimi Gibson) who (with blatant foreshadowing) tells her mom that she likes to play with the lab rabbits.

Rogers identifies the goop as some sort of marine excretion but wants to run more tests. He tells Twillinger to come back the next day. Gail feels an attraction to Twillinger and Connie urges her to pursue the matter.

Twillinger and Sheriff Peters (Gordon Jones) meet with the medical examiner at the morgue and learn that this was not a boating accident. Just kidding—they learn that the bodies have been drained of all blood and water through puncture marks. Twillinger and Jones immediately close the beaches. This leads to *Jaws* reference #2 as we cut to a local motel owner complaining to the authorities that his business will suffer as long as the beaches stay closed. This was the central idea of *Jaws'* first half, itself a reference to the famous Ibsen play, *Enemy of the People*.

Dr. Rogers continues to test the mysterious goop, putting off an impatient Twillinger who is anxious for results. One of Rogers' assistants uses a Geiger counter on the goop and it surprisingly gives off a high reading. Meanwhile, the local police visit business owner Mrs. Sims and order her to shut down her beaches. But Mrs. Sims is more concerned about her daughter Jody who has been seeing Morty, one of the men from the base. After arguing with her mother, Jody meets Morty on the beach. Jody puts on her bathing suit and urges Morty to "catch her" as she runs into the water, just like the doomed swimmer does in the opening of *Jaws* (reference #3). Morty follows her in and the two frolic in the nighttime waters. But Morty disappears. A frantic Jody calls his name. Suddenly, the girl is attacked by something beneath her in the sea, something that tugs the screaming woman under, just as Susan Backlinie was tugged under ("It hurts! It hurts!") in the famous opening sequence of *Jaws* (reference #4). Twillinger and Peters search for the missing lovers the next day and determine that their fate was the same as the diver's.

Twillinger and the scientists head out on the sea and investigate the area where the men were killed. Rogers' assistants dive down and discover a cave that has newly opened. Inside the cave they find what looks to be a giant egg. They put the egg into a net and hoist it on deck. Blake's tank gets stuck just as a huge creature attacks—the monster that has been killing everyone! It is a giant mollusk which drains the life juices from Blake. The man shrivels up before the horrified eyes of Tad Johns (Max Showalter) who escapes to the surface to tell the others what happened. In a startling scene, the monster rises out of the sea and attacks the boat (reminding me of the shark throwing itself on the deck of the Orca at the climax of *Jaws*—reference #5). Twillinger wards off the creature with a spear, poking at it like Quint did to the shark (reference #6) until finally getting rid of it when Rogers directs Twill to poke it in the eye!

The men return to shore with the egg. A sad scene follows as Connie comes to surprise her husband only to learn that he has died (it was rather rare in these films to see the aftermath of a death—the scene being even more poignant because Connie is pregnant). Twillinger notices that Gail is upset. He comforts her and she tells him how she lost her own husband.

Rogers and Twillinger debrief the men and tell them what they are dealing with. They saturate the waters with depth charges in order to destroy any more creatures and eggs. Meanwhile, Rogers keeps the remaining egg under controlled temperature. As long as the temperature is kept constant, the egg will not hatch. Of course, we know what is going to happen later. Rogers explains to the navy brass (and Sheriff Peters) that they are dealing with giant sea snails that can survive on land or sea and screens a film about modern day mollusks. He gives his theory on how they came to surface

once again and warns that if just one of these creatures should escape to the All-American Canal and hit the open water, it would multiply enough to threaten the entire human race.

Military and law enforcement join forces and plan strategies. Patrols are set up to keep watch for the creatures and make sure none of them get out of the canals. In addition, observers are stationed at each of the canal locks. Twillinger and Gail, in the meantime, go out for dinner and find they are falling for one another.

One of the patrols discovers an abandoned car. A disheveled man appears and says that the creature attacked his girl. A farmer reports that some of his cows have gone missing. No one can figure out how the creature escaped without being seen. Rogers figures there must be an underground river system by which the snails travel—and

there must be a pool where they lay their eggs. While an air search looks for the pool, Twillinger visits eccentric Mr. Dobbs (Milton Parsons) at the museum to see if there is an old map showing the underground waterway. But Dobbs can offer no help.

An old man at one of the locks calls in to report nothing unusual. Soon after, he hears splashing down in the canal. He investigates only to find a false alarm—the mysterious noises are only some young boys who have snuck in for a swim. It's pushing it but this could be *Jaws* reference #7: In Spielberg's film, two young boys with a fake shark fin, cause a panic by pretending to be the shark. In this film, the boys inadvertently cause momentary panic for the audience by making us think the monster is about to attack. The old man yells at the boys and tells them to get out of the water.

Commander Twillinger (Tim Holt) battles the sea mollusk.

Back at the lab, Sandy sneaks in to see the rabbits while Gail is occupied on the phone. Sandy feels it is too cold for the rabbits and fiddles with the temperature knob. The egg begins to thaw and hatch.

Back at the lock, the old man again hears noises and believes those naughty kids have come back again. While looking down into the canal from the bridge above and yelling at the kids below, he is attacked from behind by one of the mollusks. This is a great scary scene that always results in a jump from the audience. It is also, to me, *Jaws* reference #8. The sequence reminds me of a similar one in *Jaws*. The man in the rowboat asks Mike Brody and his friends if they need help, only to find himself the main course for the shark's dinner. Such a sequence seems very reminiscent of this moment in *The Monster That Challenged the World*. We are led to believe that children will be attacked only to have the nosy adult be the one who is killed. Both scenes work quite well in their respective pictures.

When the old man fails to report in, Twill leaves to investigate, not noticing that Mr. Dobbs has arrived with news. Dobbs chooses to wait. The locks are closed and the creature gets stuck in the mechanism. Twill is upset because they were hoping to follow the monster to its nesting area. Back at the office, Dobbs is finally able to give Twill the map he found of the waterways.

Twill and Rogers follow the map by helicopter and find a large pool covered with the goopy secretion. Twill and Casey dive in the area and find the dormant snail shells. In a tense sequence, they set charges to blow up the creatures. A stuck pin causes the two men to linger longer than they should while Rogers orders them back, over the radio. Finally, the men resurface, the explosives are blown and the monsters are killed.

Twillinger and Rogers head back to the lab where Gail and Sandy are waiting. Sandy checks on the rabbits only to find them all gone. The monster has hatched! Gail grabs her screaming daughter and they bar themselves up in a closet. The creature starts breaking down the door and Gail tells Sandy to close her eyes.

Twill finally arrives (in the nick of time) and sends Rogers for help. He distracts the monster by throwing everything at hand at the beast. Twill blows the fire extinguisher at the monster until finally it turns on him, giving Sandy and Gail a chance to escape. Twill pulls a steam hose down and burns the monster until reinforcements arrive to shoot the creature dead once and for all. The end.

The Monster That Challenged the World is definitely one of the best giant monster movies from the 1950s. It features not one but a handful of scary looking monsters. The creatures look great and are quite believable. They're not too gigantic and not always that quick, but they're big enough to be menacing to the normal person and move fast enough when they need to.

Gail (Audrey Dalton) and Sandy confront the just hatched sea mollusk.

The film is also graced with good actors. Tim Holt particularly comes off well. An underrated actor remembered mostly for his Westerns and *The Treasure of the Sierra Madre*, Holt is actually an unlikely hero and romantic lead with his paunchy physique and normal guy looks. He is set up as a hard-ass who at first comes off unlikable but throughout the film we see his tender side such as when he talks sweetly with Sandy or buys a pen from a young Hispanic boy. He is definitely the guy you want on your side and even Dr. Rogers comes to like him by the end. But Holt is at his best (and giving his all) at the end when he confronts the newly hatched monster in the lab. If you look at the expression on his face, you will see that he is truly afraid. This guy is fighting for his life (and the life of the woman he has fallen in love with) and he doesn't have much at hand to use. His expressions are ones of terror and desperation. It's actually refreshing to see the hero in one of these genre pics being afraid—it makes the film more believable. In a way, Holt's terror is a *Jaws* reference in itself (#9). In Spielberg's film, Roy Scheider's Chief Brody character is so likable and memorable because of his fear of water (or drowning as he reminds his wife) and later his fear of the shark ("We're going to need a bigger boat").

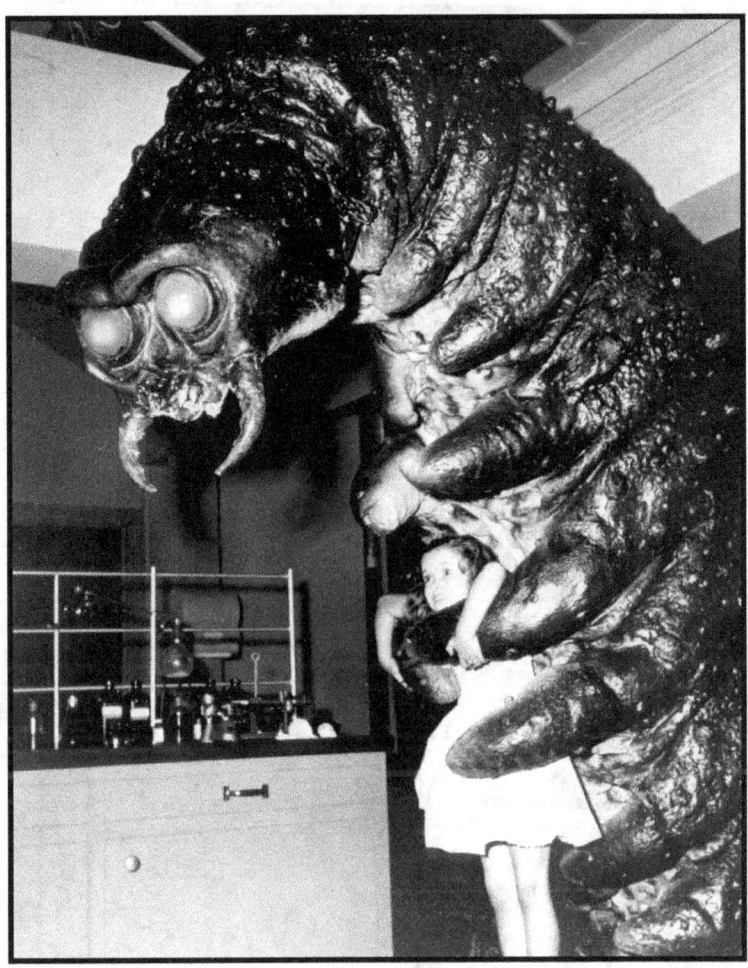

Little Sandy (Mimi Gibson) poses with the monstrous mollusk.

Hans Conreid is also very good as Dr. Rogers. With his memorable voice, we are drawn to him whenever he is on the screen. He makes a great scientist—not too obsessed with his work to crack a joke and he's willing to work alongside Twill to get the job done. Audrey Dalton is also good as the love interest. Pretty and shapely, she seems a natural match for Twill. I like the expression on her face when she sees him for the first time as she registers surprise and then attraction. She also performs well during the dinner scene where the two characters get to know each other. And we really feel for her when she and her daughter are attacked by the creature. It's difficult not to empathize when she tells little Sandy to close her eyes so she won't see the creature coming to kill them. Max Showalter (aka Casey Adams) as assistant Johns does a fine job as well. He deftly expresses the guilt he feels over the death of his colleague. And Gordon Jones, a veteran of Abbott and Costello films, is reliable as always as the sheriff.

The film also works well because it expertly fuses suspense with lighter scenes of comic relief. The monster attacks are tensely frightening—especially on the divers and the old man at the lock. As mentioned, Holt's final battle with the newly hatched snail is exciting and scary. But the best example of the film's suspense occurs just before that when Sandy and Gail are menaced by the snail. The monster starts breaking through the wooden door getting closer and closer. Meanwhile, the film cuts to Twill and Rogers casually driving back to the lab after disposing of the beasts. They are rather proud of themselves and they seem to be taking their time. At one point in the cross-cutting, Rogers asks Twill if he wants to grab something to eat. We in the audience want to cry out, "No, you idiots! Get back to the lab!" Luckily for Gail (and us) Twill is not hungry.

The film abounds in light comic moments that never fail to bring a smile. I particularly like how Twill's secretary is always on the phone with her mother—even during the height of the emergency situation. There's also a funny cut that occurs when the Sheriff tells Twill that watching the locks reminds him of a stakeout that occurred a while back where nothing happened. The film immediately cuts to two officers in a patrol car with one of the cops complaining and mentioning the same stakeout! Other light moments include Twill telling Gail on the phone that

he is hungry and would like to have dinner with her, while he's actually eating, and Mr. Dobbs' continual obsession with proposition 14A. There's also a nice moment of black comedy when the medical examiner offers Twill and the Sheriff cold sandwiches—which he's been keeping on one of the slabs.

Unlike some other genre flicks, *The Monster That Challenged the World* features scientists, police and military all working together to stop the creatures. It's refreshing to see this cooperation and there's no doubt they will succeed in stopping the snails by working together. *Jaws* has a similar cooperation, but here is my own "English Major" theory being applied here. I always felt that Hooper thematically represents book learning with his degrees and his fancy equipment. Quint to me represents street smarts, wise through his experiences on the sea and as a fisherman. Brody is the Everyman. He naturally ends up facing the shark alone and defeats it only by combining book smarts with street smarts. Neither Hooper nor Quint could do it alone but Brody gets the idea to aim his gun (street smarts) at the compressed air tank (which Hooper explained to him—book learning) in the shark's mouth. Boom! The shark is killed by the Everyman, the one we identify with the most.

I am still surprised that the similarities between *The Monster That Challenged the World* and *Jaws* have not been mentioned and delved into further. Bill Warren, in his seminal *Keep Watching the Skies*, almost picks up on it. Within his surprisingly brief entry on the film, he mentions that the creatures, if they got loose, would be no more menacing than sharks, yet he, too, fails to make a logical connection with *Jaws*. Maybe they are not so obvious. Maybe they are akin to the Lincoln-Kennedy assassination coincidences in that they are just that—coincidences.

Whatever the case, the cinematic fascination with sharks remains at an all-time high (Discovery Channel still has its highest ratings during its annual Shark Week, and such films as *Open Water, Megalodon* and *Dark Waters* are proliferating on video store shelves). It's only a matter of time until *The Monster That Challenged the World* is rediscovered and movie fans realize that it's one (s)hell of a motion picture!

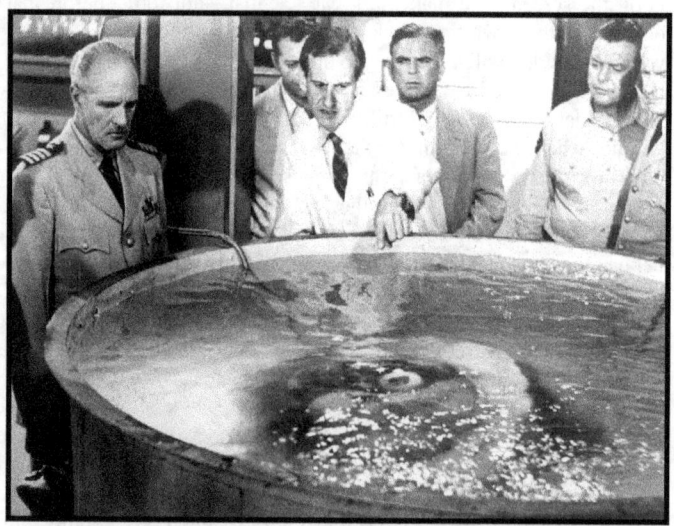

Dr. Rogers (Hans Conreid) watches as a sea monster hatches.

Ratings: Excellent 4; Good 3; Fair 2; Poor 1

The Ghost
Dead Eyes of London
Movies: *Ghost*: 2.5;
Dead Eyes: 3.5; Disc: 3.0
Retromedia/Image

Fred Olen Ray's fledgling Retromedia Entertainment, now distributed by Image Entertainment, makes this small indie an even larger indie company. Unlike Image, Warner Bros. and Blue Underground, etc., Retromedia does not digitally restore its releases, so audiences are bound to see scratches, end of reel gaps and jump cuts, etc. However the prints selected are generally in very fine condition. This DVD double-bill replicates the American theatrical double billing of these two rare features and becomes a nostalgic treat for fans.

First off, *The Ghost*, directed by Riccardo Freda (billed as Robert Hampton for American distribution), illustrates both the strengths and the flaws inherent in the Euro-Gothic genre. Freda, Mario Bava's mentor, creates a widescreen Techni-color scarefest dripping in moody cinematography. Often times the camera becomes almost another character as camera explores the shadowy corridors of the spooky mansion, the underground burial vaults, etc. To me the balance is slightly askew as too much mood equals tedium, but connoisseurs of Euro horror seem to enjoy such diversions. Once again the plot is predictable but is always secondary to the cinematography and the intense psychologically driven characters. And by 1963, when this movie was made, Barbara Steele was a horror film icon (although in *The Ghost* she seems too thin with overdone eye makeup and a big hair wig that tends to draw attention away from her expressive mouth and eyes). The plot involves Dr. Hitchcock (Leonard G. Elliott), his wife Margaret (Steele) and Hitchcock's doctor Charles (Peter Baldwin). Hitchcock suffers from a degenerative neurological disease, and as treatment, the physician Charles administers poison, with the antidote quickly following. However, Margaret and Charles are having an affair, so Hitchcock is quickly killed off with the poison (minus the antidote). Soon a cat and mouse game involving Hitchcock's riches and where they are hidden leads to suspicion and betrayal, especially when Hitchcock's missing gems and jewelry are found falling out of Charles' medical bag. At the same time ghostly apparitions occur, swinging chandeliers, flying chess pieces and even the ghastly return of a decaying Hitchcock, ultimately prompting Margaret's murder of her lover using a straight razor as she slashes his face, arms, body, producing a wonderful shot where his blood drips down the camera lens as the viewer watches the hateful intensity in the face of Margaret. Of course it turns out Hitchcock is not dead, and using his faithful house servant as accomplice, Hitchcock has concocted a plan for revenge by turning the smoldering passion between murderous lovers into mistrust and ultimately murder. But in the best tradition of treachery (based upon *The Pardoner's Tale* from *The Canterbury Tales*), in celebration, the good doctor drinks poison gin and dies a slow, tortuous death as his wife also dies from poison, but she laughs hysterically as his perfect plan backfires and the police arrive. *The Ghost*, for me, disappoints as the plot is transparent, the mood and cinematography overdone and the characters little more than stereotypes. Better examples of this style of Euro horror exist, and in a movie running slightly over 90 minutes, more sequences of visitations from the dead are needed to generate horror. The slightly letterboxed print has *not* been enhanced for 16:9 monitors and the print has its shares of scratches and jump cuts. The color on this DVD is quite intense but fails to capture the intensity of the original Technicolor print.

The second feature, *Dead Eyes of London*, is a black and white, letterboxed (again, *not* enhanced for 16:9 monitors) German *krimi* film based upon an Edgar Wallace story (similar in tone to the Dr. Mabuse films). While these can best be considered crime/mysteries, their style seems to predate the Italian giallo film and contain distinct horror elements. The film is a remake of the Bela Lugosi film *The Human Monster*, detail-

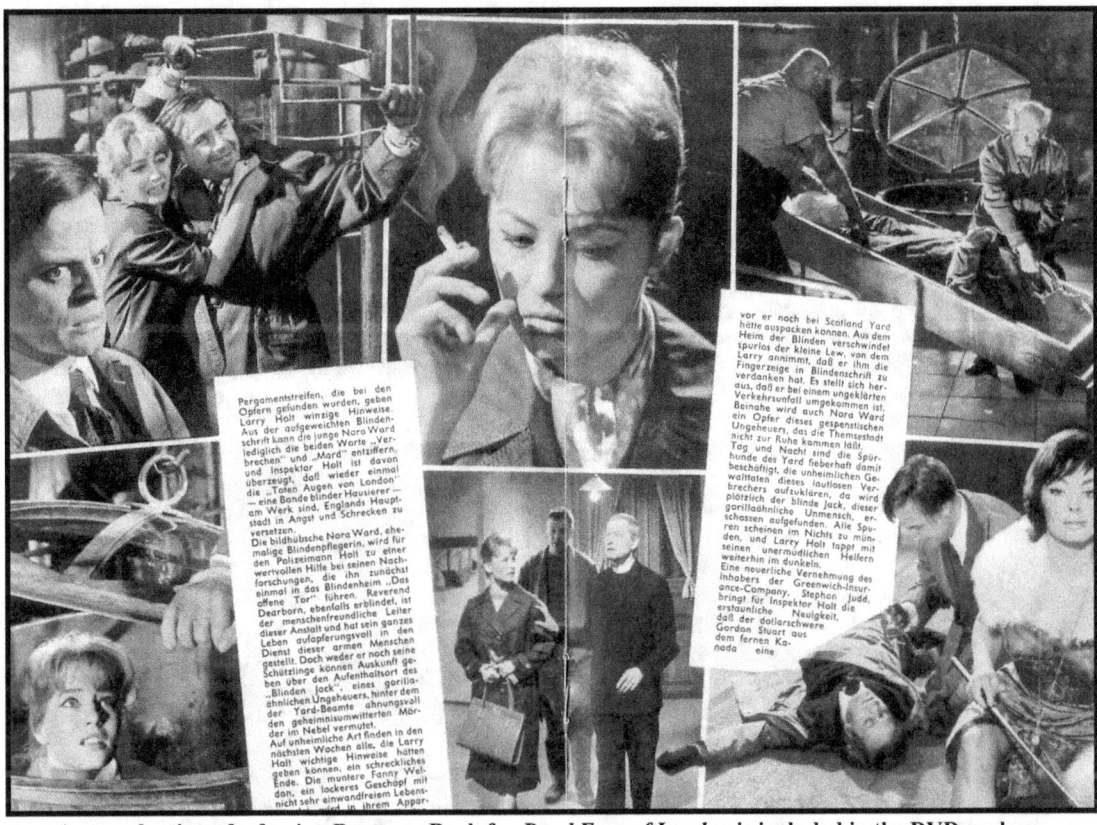

A reproduction of a foreign Program Book for *Dead Eyes of London* is included in the DVD package.

ing the deceptive world of misplaced identity, insurance company fraud, a missionary for the blind used as a criminal front and corpses floating around the riverfront. Director Alfred Vohrer became an expert in helming this type of film, and stylistically, *Dead Eyes of London* contains some fabulous sequences of terror and suspense. The icon figure of Ady Berber as Blind Jack becomes a central image of 1960s Euro horror, dominating poster art and submitting a spooky Tor Johnson-esque performance as the blind, hairy-arm brute who claims human victims in the fog-shrouded city streets. Even his death with his massive body rolled down a hill at the garbage dump, is disturbing with his blind white eyes staring upward. And we also get an early Klaus Kinski performance as a creepy gangster who dies when he is shoved through a glass window and falls screaming to his death.

The movie shines when the convoluted plot moves away from the talky investigative stage and instead depends upon visuals to create a gripping web of suspense. In one terrific sequence our police hero goes into a room and hears a mechanical voice from behind him ordering him *not* to turn around and to approach and open a cabinet. The investigator realizes opening the cabinet door will spell his death, so as he reaches toward the handle, he quickly whips out his revolver and turns around to find a tape recorder blasting out the message. Moving aside, opening the door, gunfire blasts radiate from within the TV screen housed inside the cabinet, and the policeman plays dead to see who appears. Such a sequence is gripping and cleverly executed and suggests James Bond.

By the movie's end, the clergyman in charge of the home for the blind is revealed to be the chief villain, who threatens the young damsel in distress by forcing her to sign documents leaving all her worldly possessions to the mission upon her death (she is due to inherit a fortune). When she refuses, she is placed into a drowning chamber that is quickly filled with surging water, as her boyfriend remains tied up within screaming distance. When he finally frees himself, he has to face an acetylene torch and the appearance of a second villain to save the day.

Even the comic relief (assistant to chief investigator) of Eddi Arent is inspired, the seemingly feminine assistant investigator saving his boss with his excellent marksmanship. The original source material here, most likely a good contrast black and white 16mm print, is quite acceptable. The print has its share of jump cuts (only one annoying) and a few scratches, but the subtlety of mood and photography is maintained.

Retromedia Entertainment creates a nice double feature package that highlights rare Euro horror productions with a good presentation. Extras include a reproduction of the original German pressbook for *Dead Eyes of London*, trailers for both movies and a still gallery for *Dead Eyes of London*.

Ghost of Dragstrip Hollow
Ghost in the Invisible Bikini
Movies:
Dragstrip Hollow: 2.5;
Invisible Bikini: 2.0;
Disc: 3.5
[MGM Midnite Movies DVD]

At first I thought this Midnite Movies double feature was a lousy coupling, but after seeing both features back to back, I can see a glimmer of genius in their selection. *Ghost of Dragstrip Hollow* was released in 1959 and *Ghost in the Invisible Bikini* was released only seven years later in 1966, both products of American International's exploitation attack on youthful movie viewers. However, *Dragstrip Hollow* closed out the decade that featured crisp black and white B productions and bargain basement monsters created in part by Paul Blaisdell, ending the *I Was a Teenage* — barrage of movies and ending the fascination on J.D. and drag racing teens. In fact, while the She Creature makes a spooky return, even dancing and partying at the movie's conclusion, even better is the on-film appearance of Paul Blaisdell who takes off his monster head and whines at the camera in a clever comic bit stating how the insenitive studio heads rejected him for *Horrors of the Black Museum* (inaugurating the new era of color and widescreen AIP horrors) after he terrified audiences for close to a decade. Only American International would include such a dose of reality in an otherwise teenage fantasy.

Following the money-making formula, *Ghost of Dragstrip Hollow* features teens that belong to a drag racing club who are into engines and racing, who are typically good kids, but kids misunderstood by their parents. Even a few girls with bullet bras and tight-fitting jeans belong to the group, including leading teen Lois (Jody Fair), and everyone in the club is distressed that they will be losing their garage/clubhouse in a few weeks. An adult reporter working on a story becomes their sympathetic ally, proving not all adults are jerks, like their parents always seem to be (in a cute, loving way). Even though the reporter considers himself a square, his intelligence comes to the rescue of the teens more than once. Soon an eccentric old lady Mrs. Abernathy (Dorothy Neumann), who stays at the home of Lois and her parents for two weeks, allows the kids to use her old house as their base of operations, if they can get rid of the ghosts and the She Creature. But worldly Lois, when sitting on her daddy's knees, is told she is on the verge of womanhood, she gloats and beams, "Haven't you noticed, I've arrived!" When daddy asks if she had *that* talk with her mother, she responds, yes, and she brags of all the things she taught her mom. But basically she is a good, intelligent kid who feels more comfy with hot rods than

hot romances, even though instead of having a catfight with her catty rival, she challenges the vixen to a drag race that always ends with her father grounding her and she having to pay the fine for violating the rules of the club. This movie establishes the fact that even teens have rules and standards.

Abernathy's pet parrot's over-dubbed voice shenanigans provide some of the silliest laughter of the film ("Polly want a cracker?"… "What the hell would I want with a cracker??!!"). Mrs. Abernathy with her eccentric nature and sense of wild fun again demonstrates that old, old adults can be just as wild and crazy as the younger teens. Of course the haunted house is played more for laughs than chills, and during the spook ball, when the house band plays "Mustang," the kids all dressed in their finest Halloween customs dancing in wild abandon, the movie resembles *American Bandstand* more than AIP horror. Finally the house ghost, resembling Jonathan Haze, glumly leaves the house, "driven out by the rock and roll jam," as the kids dance away ending with the end title "The Endest Man," as the band's vocalist yells "charge."

Ghost in the Invisible Bikini, although produced just seven years later by AIP, is actually one generation ahead of the image of 1950s teens. Now *Horrors of the Black Museum* has led to all of AIP's movies being filmed in garish color and widescreen, but this time, with a larger B budget, featuring fading stars Boris Karloff (as the Corpse Hiram Stokely), Basil Rathbone (Mr. Ripper) and silent film star Francis X. Bushman as the butler, with TV star Jesse White along for the ride as Ripper's flunky. The story, sillier than silly, features Susan Hart (the main squeeze of AIP president Jim Nicholson) as the now dead but former circus star "girl in the invisible bikini" who appears to movie audiences (she is invisible to the onscreen cast) in blue tint with the top and bottom of her bikini totally transparent. She is the helper of recently dead Stokely who must commit one good deed in order to go to heaven and regain his youth (so he can entertain the Ghost).

So we have the team of villains, masterminded by evil Ripper, whose sexy daughter Sinistra (Quinn O'Hara), a teen built like a brick shithouse whose prominent glasses make her geeky yet sexy, seduces and tries to murder youthful heirs to the hidden household treasure (pushing them off rocky bluffs; however, without her glasses, she actually tumbles stone statues instead). Added to the mix we have Eric Von Zipper (Harvey Lembeck) and his motorcycle gang The Rats who join the hi-jinks trying to find the hidden treasure, and we have the lovable teens headed by Tommy Kirk and Deborah Wally reacting to the festivities in the (once again) haunted house. We see adults are not to be trusted and that the kids are the true heroes with the right morals and courage. Sinistra, evil daughter of Mr. Ripper, is the major exception, but with that name she must not have many friends.

Like an update of *Ghost of Dragstrip Hollow*, we have a counterpart to Mrs. Aberthany, here Patsy Kelly as the elderly and slightly eccentric Myrtle Forbush. Instead of drag racers we have motorcyclists, and under the control of their "boss" Von Zipper, the slapstick gets thick and gooey. Yet Harvey Lembeck's persona becomes one of the strong points of the entire AIP Beach Party series, of which this movie is an extension. Instead of some faceless house band from *Ghost of Dragstrip Hollow*, we have the immortal Bobby Fuller Four who perform solo and with Nancy Sinatra and others. However, we are not treated to their biggest hit, "I Fought the Law."

And poor Boris, he is forced to rise from a coffin and make intelligent conversation with the over-

mugging Susan Hart, who does look mighty cute in her teensy bikini. Both Tommy Kirk and Deborah Wally's parents owned carnivals and were swindled by Stokely, and now as his good deed he aims to leave his inheritance to the two young heirs and Mrs. Forbush (his mistress) to make amends for his evil past. However shady lawyer Mr. Ripper has his own sights on the fortune. In fact, once Sinistra whacks the golden statue of Cupid who fires his arrows, the treasure is released from a chandelier above. While everyone fights over the money, Mr. Ripper comes armed with a rifle and demands all the cash, but the Ghost literally blows him up, and in the only truly hilarious sequence in the ridiculous movie, a little cartoon of an angel Rathbone, plucking his little harp, rises toward heaven. And poor, poor Boris, who was promised as part of his reward that he would regain his youth so he could get together with the sexy Ghost, discovers that he is restored to his youth—his childhood youth, and that he once again will ascend to heaven alone.

The movie ends with a defeated Von Zipper asking "why me, why me again" as the rock and roll credits come up on screen and the entire cast dances the night away, happy as larks, the music and dancing reminding us more than a little of the similar conclusion to *Ghost of Dragstrip Hollow*.

Amazingly, both films offer similar takes of comic horror romps geared toward a teen audience, but each film is formulated to appeal to a slightly different teen audience. Focus on the world of teens and their problems, throw in some aging adults as villains, but also offer some eccentric adults and one or two oldsters who become friends of the teens and their causes. Present the young adults as mild rebels but make them also responsible and willing to make amends for their errors. Offer lots of rock music and scantily clad couples wiggling and squirming to the music. Add a little spooky haunted house action, but drape the horror in large dabs of slapstick and emphasize the fun.

Both teen romps (*Ghost of Dragstrip Hollow* and *Ghost in the Invisible Bikini*) are basically mediocre/bad movies that can be redeemed merely by their infectious sense of harmless fun. Both films succeed as mindless drive-in theater fodder. Incredibly the stark black and white fine grain 35mm print used for *Ghost of Dragstrip Hollow* is exceptional, as is the bold soundtrack. Even better is the deeply saturated Pathé color widescreen print used for *Ghost in the Invisible Bikini* that is exceptionally sharp. Both films are not worthy of their terrific presentation here (even *Ghost* is enhanced for 16:9 monitors). Neither film is the best AIP offered during either decade, but with a stunning presentation here, both films deserve one more viewing to remind us of lost innocence.

Dracula Has Risen from the Grave
Movie: 3.0; Disc: 3.5
[Warner Home Video]

It used to be that Anchor Bay introduced all the best latter-day Hammer productions to DVD with fantastic visuals and sound, rounded out with a host of extras. Of late Warner Home Video has taken up the banner, releasing Hammer horror classics to DVD with very solid original source material (the exception being *Horror of Dracula*, which was released with a gorgeous looking print, but presented in the wrong aspect ratio with tops of heads shamefully cropped). *Dracula Has Risen from the Grave*, the third Dracula entry from Hammer starring Christopher Lee, is here presented with an unblemished 35mm print that is vibrant featuring full-bodied sound. While the original film was printed in Technicolor, the DVD falls slightly short of that color density, but it is one beautiful print nonetheless.

While *Horror of Dracula* is the greatest Hammer horror classic, with Christopher Lee-less *Brides of Dracula* running only slightly behind, the true Hammer debate is whether *Dracula—Prince of Darkness* or *Dracula Has Risen from the Grave* is the second or third best Lee entry. While each film has its share of flaws and praiseworthy points, a recent viewing of both films settles the dispute for me—*Dracula Has Risen from the Grave* is third best. And here's why. Freddie Francis was truly a marvelous guest at FANEX and is infinitely funny in a very dry way, but his forte will always be cinematography, and even though Arthur Grant shot the movie, Francis' touch is evident everywhere. The inspired use of filters, muted

coloring and the expansive use of the rooftop sets make the movie appear more expensive than it really is. However, Francis' direction and sense of vampires as the undead pales in comparison to Terence Fisher's direction. Even without saying one word in *Prince of Darkness*, Christopher Lee's ungodly presence is mesmerizing and particularly creepy. In *Risen from the Grave* Lee's Count Dracula comes off more as a thug, a bully, a one-dimensional caricature that seems far too worldly and not supernatural. Even the pivotal sequence where Count Dracula gets stalked in the coffin and pulls the splinter from his chest is more a marvelous special effect than a riveting sequence. For contrast, think of any of the stakings enacted by Peter Cushing in *Horror of Dracula*… those sequences resonate long after leaving the theater. The script is mundane in *Dracula Has Risen from the Grave*, and most of the performances, with one or two exceptions, are journeyman at best (compare Rupert Davies' Monsignor to Peter Cushing's Van Helsing or even Andrew Keir's vampire slayer from *Dracula—Prince of Darkness*).

Besides the cinematography and inspired use of sets, *Dracula Has Risen from the Grave* features a sensual and perky performance from Veronica Carlson, one of Hammer's most endearing horror heroines. With her aura of innocence and lovely legs and hair, she becomes a victim that inspires audience sympathy and concern. Her sexy sequences with Christopher Lee become the most involving in the entire movie, and she provides the sexuality to Lee's undead performance. Equally effective is bad girl Barbara Ewing whose ample cleavage makes her the ideal victim of Dracula. Michael Ripper, again playing the barkeep, submits one of his usual superb supporting performances.

With only a thea-trical trailer as extra, Warner Home Video takes a back seat to Anchor Bay as far as supplemental extras go. At minimum, we should have been offered an audio commentary track with Veronica Carlson and Christopher Lee, if not Freddie Francis himself. But while the movie is formula, *Dracula Has Risen from the Grave* showcases second rung Hammer to absolute perfection.

Freaks
Movie: 3.0; Disc: 3.5
[Warner Home Video]

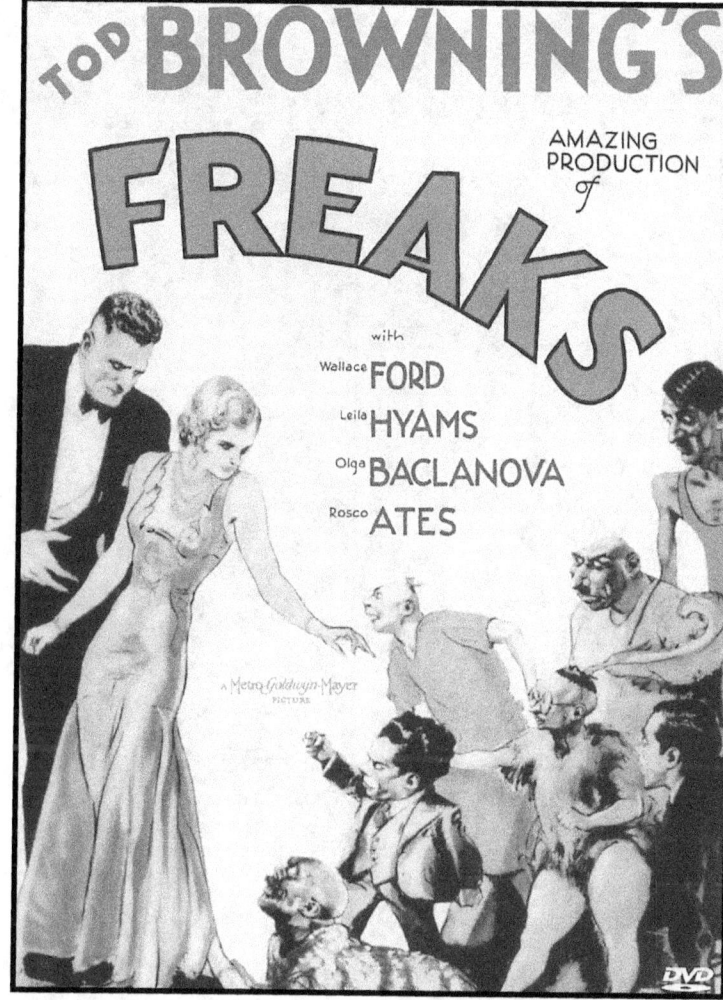

What are we to make of Tod Browning's *Freaks* in 2005? While *Freaks* may well be the most mainstream sideshow exploitation movie ever made, it still shows the shortcomings of director Tod Browning, even though this may very well be his most consistent movie artistically. While such a menagerie of human oddities may have shocked back in the early 1930s, today, their sight brings curiosity and sympathy, not revulsion. The message that the ever-strong community of "gooble, gooble, we accept her... one of us" conveys is easily understood, and the fact that the healthy looking humans are the savages, the true freaks, is now cliché today. That doesn't deny this movie its power for portraying a subculture in a strong light.

While the movie might be criticized for leering and lingering far too long upon these human curiosities (a long, protracted sequence depicting the human torso lighting a match with his teeth is just one example), such sequences can be interpreted in two ways. And while the carnival sideshow setting reeks of exploitation, the major plot demonstrating the love affair of one little person's attraction toward a beautiful full-sized woman is simply emotionally draining (due to her mocking his kindnesses and insulting his kind). Of course this leads to the final rain-soaked, lightning-lighted climax where the human oddities, now framed in a horror movie setting, descend upon and savagely kill those humans who mocked them. Unfortunately these innocents are finally depicted as monsters that show their true colors in the darkness. For me it is difficult to get the handle if Tod Browning was being compassionate or exploitative in his depiction of this subculture. The film, rather slowly paced, has several pivotal sequences that shake the rafters, but overall, the film is never better than simply good.

After decades of deteriorating prints, this Warner Home Video DVD seems complete and flawless, offering a pristine presentation with good density and solid sound. While the print still has some grain and some pops and hiss in the soundtrack, the film has not looked nor sounded this good in decades. Extras include commentary by David J. Skal and an informative documentary featuring Skal and members of the carnival/sideshow circuit. The film's Prologue warning has been restored, and three alternative endings are shown (actually variations of the same basic ending). While *Freaks* has always distanced me because of its wavering tone that does not clearly identify the movie's intent, I still am amazed by the film's sometimes stunning cinematography and enthralled by its emotional plotline. And it is about time we can finally see *Freaks* as it was meant to be seen.

Van Helsing
Movie: 3.0; Disc: 3.5
[Universal Home Video]

Universal created and presented their classic movie monsters during the decade of the 1930s. They recycled these same classic monster icons into monster rallies during the decade of the 1940s. During the decade of the 1950s and 1950s, Hammer Film Productions of England recreated these same monsters in vibrant color and oozing sexuality for new generations. And now 40 years after Hammer, Universal itself has tried to resurrect its franchise monsters for a new generation raised on non-stop action/adventure and CGI special effects. What Hammer did so beautifully back then, Universal fumbles today.

Van Helsing is truly a curiosity, a movie that features some marvelous sequences but a movie that ultimately ruins the mix due to overkill and condescending to lowest common denominator tastes. It is apparent that Stephen Summers movies, at least before shooting commences, are movies created and produced by committee, perhaps allowing Summers to become director only if he acquiesces to the committee's vision. It does not seem to matter if he screenwrites and directs the movie, because the final film is ultimately compromised by this committee mentality.

For instance, the movie's strength, besides its vast richness of Gothic sets and meticulous set production design, are the human monster performances (not CGI) of Richard Roxburgh as Count Dracula, Shuler Hensley as Frankenstein's Monster and perennial Kevin J. O'Connor as Igor (not Ygor, strangely enough). Even while performing under silly hairdos (Roxburgh) or tons of makeup and costume (Hensley and O'Connor), it is the human element that makes their performances special. They somehow are allowed to connect as human beings, cursed as they may be, but human beings with souls, yearnings, passions and needs. Count Dracula, whose performance is based upon its musicality and his rhythmic dancing in each and every sequence (even mimicking Fred Astaire's walking on the ceiling from *Royal Wedding*), speaks of the loneliness of immortality and his longing to bring offspring into his depraved world (the cheap imitation of the egg chamber from *Aliens* undermines such a sensitive plotline). Kevin J. O'Connor's Igor, still cruel and evil, has some of the funniest lines (along with Friar David Wenham) that speak to the heart of the Universal mythos. When asked why he tortures and is so cruel, he answers matter-of-factly, "It's what I do." That line is funny yet still poignant, because in the Universal Monster Mythos, characters such as Ygor and Fritz and others are evil simply because their presence is needed to be cruel, as their only reason for being. But it is Shuler Hensley's performance as Frankenstein's Monster that steals the show. In his battered football player body, with its convertible skull that pops open to reveal his glowing brain, Hensley's humanity and self-sacrifice registers his pivotal line of dialogue, in every sequence in which he appears—"I want to live!!!" Here we have the most pathetic Monster performance since Karloff's where we can really observe the craft of acting bellowing out from prosthetic makeup. We can feel the Monster's pain and lust for life, and when the creature is constantly tortured and shackled, we can sense that his passion to live is stronger than any chains or boulder of ice in which he is encased. Quite simply, Hensley is the heart and soul of this production.

It is during the middle sections that Stephen Summers is able to generate some sense of artistic resonance and characterizations that involve the viewing audience, that make us care as we used to care about Universal monsters four decades ago, or seven decades ago, when actors such as Boris Karloff, Bela Lugosi, Lon Chaney, Jr., Peter Cushing and Christopher Lee created performances that chilled our bones, but gave performances that revealed human longing. Yes, the makeup was always way cool, but it was the human soul underneath that brought the monsters to vivid life.

In Universal's monster rally *Van Helsing*, Stephen Summers is ultimately undermined by his "too much is too much" ethic, where state-of-the-art special effects become the be-all and end-all, and such effects only end up becoming far too silly

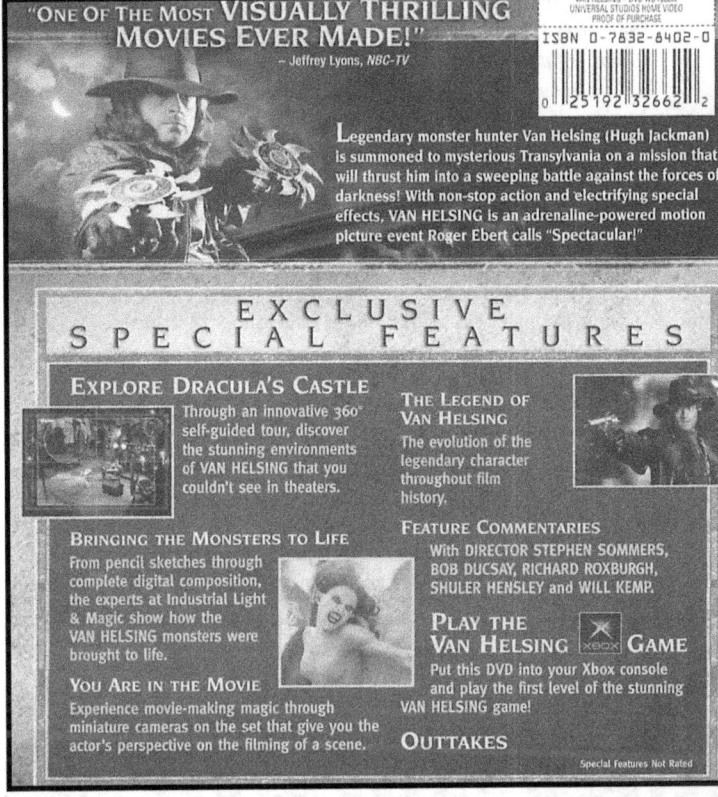

and cartoonish. Universal (through directors such as James Whale, Tod Browning, Edgar Ulmer, etc.) taught us that a cartoonish setting is only effective if the inhabitants of that fairy story world resonate with the truth of human compassion. Universal in the 1930s and 1940s knew this. Hammer in the 1950s and 1960s knew this as well. But in the world of today's cinema, when movies are

no longer visions of one individual but the commercial-minded visions of many, that cartoon world spins out of control and exists only for its own sense of playful video game reality. Its human inhabitants are left to flounder, stumble and fight for a few glorified moments of realistic emotion and passions. While it is great to have the classic Universal monsters back, putting them in a demonic Ray Harryhausen world of visual delight only undermines their battered and broken humanity.

Interestingly, in a telephone conversation with Kevin J. O'Connor, he shared that Stephen Summers' favorite Universal horror movie was *Abbott and Costello Meet Frankenstein* where Count Dracula is the monster leader and whose goal is to revive the Frankenstein Monster to do his bidding. In *Van Helsing* Summers makes Dracula the monster leader once again.

Extras focus upon documentaries that explain special effects; however, the blooper reel and the History of Van Helsing in the Cinema are first rate as well.

The Night Stalker
The Night Strangler
Movie: *Stalker*: 3.0;
Strangler: 2.5
[MGM Home Entertainment]

Amazingly, in 1972 the made-for-TV movie *The Night Stalker* broke all records and became, for its time, the most successful TV movie of all time. It also become Dan Curtis' shining moment as either producer and/or director.

Running a scant 75 minutes, echoing the similar running times of the classic Universals of the 1930s, *The Night Stalker* mixed chilling horror, outrageous characterizations and political satire into a perfect brew of mainstream Hollywood entertainment, produced on a budget.

While the movie is creepy and eerie, it is seldom truly scary (yes, we have two or three in-your-face shock sequences, but this is not the same as the classic atmospheric scare). We have glitzy Vegas showgirls walk down alleyways and get grabbed by outstretched arms, and we have a door burst open revealing a fang-barring vampire behind it, but the direction, for me, is always journeyman caliber, never inspired. But for a made-for-TV movie, journeyman is quite adequate.

What makes *The Night Stalker* so inspired is its wealth of wonderful performances, chiefly anchored by Darren McGavin's inspired turn as cocky, loner journalist Carl Kolchak, the man who is willing to cross anyone to get at the truth and to get the truth published. What he doesn't understand is that politicos never desire the truth to be published, because the general citizen cannot possibly handle the truth. So those who wield the power dictate what "truth" to publish, and Kolchak, seemingly hardened, is basically a idealistic babe in the woods. But his self-righteous rants, of the little reporter who wishes he could be heard, inspire all of us who wish we could stand up to and defeat those in power who crush the little guy without thought of consequence.

Also, Barry Atwater at Janos Shorzeny makes a very impressive vampire, but often his physical prowess in encounters with the police, where he stands up to an army of cops and escapes flipping over chairs, humans and furniture, tends to destroy his sense of mystery and undeadness. Far better are the sequences in the old house near the end where Janos has a female victim tied and gagged and is draining her daily for her blood supply. At least the modern Vegas setting is momentarily replaced by a Gothic set piece that is more familiar as a vampire's lair. Even the quasi *Horror of Dracula* ending, with the sunlight holding the vampire paralyzed while Kolchak and buddy stake the vampire on the stairs, pales in contrast to the Hammer classic. But the aftermath of this vampire's destruction, with Kolchak sent packing out of town, is the film's actual blood-letting and metaphorical shafting.

The Richard Matheson screenplay does a marvelous job in updating the vampire mythos, and the beginning and ending frame, having Kolchak speak directly to his audience as he records the course of events into his mini-recorder, draws the viewer immediately into the story. For 75 minutes of TV, *The Night Stalker* deserves credit as a modern classic and worthy revitalizer of the vampire cinema.

While I originally preferred *The Night Strangler* (the sequel, again returning Kolchak to investigate a series of strangulations near Underground Seattle) to the original, upon subsequent viewings, I have to give the nod to the original. However, the 1973 sequel is almost as good, and at 90 minutes it still sustains interest throughout.

For the sequel Darren McGavin sports better-styled (and lighter) hair, but he still wears his seersucker suit and plays the role of arrogant coward to the hilt. Again working with his gruff newspaper editor Simon Oakland, the rapport between the formerly bitter adversaries is more close-knit in the sequel as both are under the power of newspaper magnate John Carradine, who ultimately has both men fired and on the road by the final scene.

The Night Strangler follows the formula of its predecessor much too closely and we have beautiful young women murdered and their blood drained as a hundred-year-old doctor, in the best tradition of *The Man in Half Moon Street/The Man Who Could Cheat Death* uses a blood serum to maintain immortality. His formula is flawed and he needs a new infusion of blood and formula every 21 years. Richard Anderson plays the fiend, but he only has one sequence near the end of the movie where he gets to perform and establish his character. In every other sequence he is merely depicted as a shadowy figure who preys on innocent victims in the foggy streets of Seattle. And quite stupidly, before he takes his potion, he allows Kolchak time to throw a projectile at the bubbling vial and break it, thus

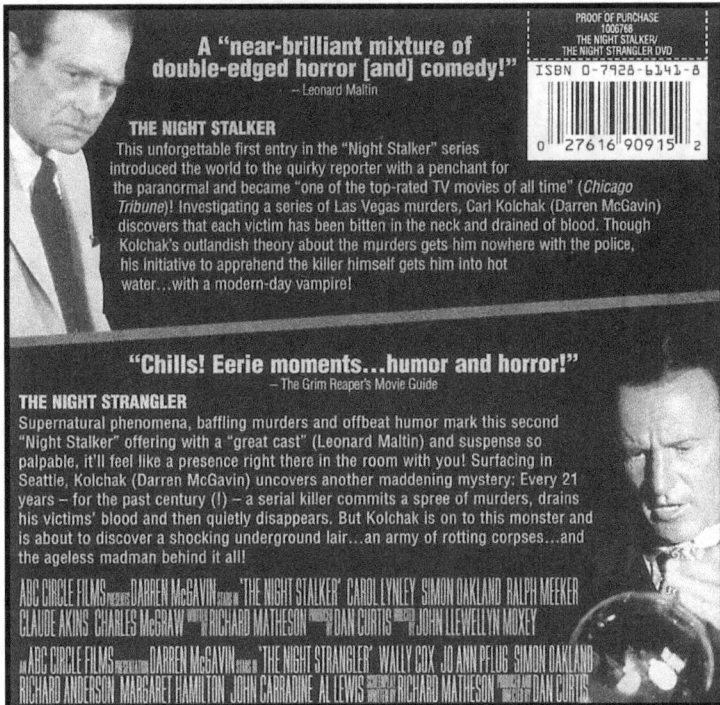

destroying the formula. *The Night Strangler* did not inspire another made-for-TV movie, but it helped to inspire the TV series that featured Kolchak fighting monsters, zombies and other creatures of the night. While the quality of the series never came close to equaling the quality of these two movies, it established that Darren McGavin struck gold near the end of his career playing a lovable curmudgeon down-on-his-luck newspaper reporter that audiences saw as the definitive underdog.

While Dan Curtis used the veteran director John Moxey for *The Night Stalker*, he used himself to direct *The Night Strangler*, but the differences in directorial style are hardly noticeable, as the movies complement one another quite perfectly in both style and casting. In the original Curtis hired old vets Ralph Meeker, Claude Akins and Charles McGraw, Kent Smith and Elishu Cook, Jr. for supporting roles. In the sequel he employed John Carradine, Wally Cox and Margaret Hamilton. As mentioned, the Richard Matheson screenplays follow the same patterns. And the basic look of both films is similar, placing Gothic monsters, demons from the past, in glitzy urban settings.

As extras on this double-feature DVD presentation we have onscreen interviews with Dan Curtis about both his commercial and artistic success with these back-to-back telemovies. Both movies are presented full screen and feature exceptionally clean and colorful prints. Looking back upon both films we can see what an exceptional contribution Darren McGavin made to horror cinema with his eccentric character of Carl Kolchak, and those performances and these two movies still stand tall over 30 years later.

Dawn of the Dead
Movie: 3.5; Disc: 3.5
[Universal Home Video]

It's now been almost 30 years since director George Romero unleashed his epic zombie movie *Dawn of the Dead* theatrically, and most of the surviving cast have been on the convention circuit the last few years. Romero, after two decades, returned to direct his fourth zombie entry, *Land of the Dead*. So was it necessary to remake *Dawn of the Dead* now?

To be quite candid, most of the recent remakes and clones of 1970s horror classics have been quite successful—*Texas Chainsaw Massacre, House of 10,000 Corpses, 28 Days Later, Shaun of the Dead, Cabin Fever, Final Exit*. However, I feel that Zack Snyder's remake of *Dawn of the Dead* is the finest American mainstream modern horror movie in the past three years. It does borrow the basic premise from Romero's original and recreates the suburban mall setting as the major set piece for the action and gore. However, Snyder's vision develops as an original vision, one that is at best described as being influenced by the Romero movie. Myself, I found *Dawn of the Dead* to be Romero's most excessive and least successful in the entire zombie trilogy, so I have no problem saying I found the new *Dawn of the Dead* to be superior to the old.

We have all the ingredients of a great horror movie at work here: a movie based upon solid characterization and effective acting, well directed sequences that slowly build up to the horror and don't hit us over the head with makeup effects that shock simply on the basis of oozing blood, a great sense of claustrophobia, surprises, some necessary and never overdone humor and sympathy for the cast of characters. Running almost two hours long, *Dawn of the Dead* never sags in the middle or spends too much time doing any one thing too often.

Anchored by a professional cast featuring Sarah Polley as the lead (know mostly for her TV work in *Anne of Green Gables*), along with policeman Ving Rhames as the titular leader of the band of survivors, the supporting cast of virtual unknowns shines, featuring everyone from psycho mall security guards to Best Buy TV salesmen, but every character evolves, they change, and this is a strength of the movie. One character, seemingly so trigger-happy and caring only for himself, gradually warms up to the group and eventually sacrifices his own life for the welfare of everyone. Another character with absolutely no experience in military or survival skills slowly be-comes one of the dominant leaders based upon his quick thinking, common sense and compassion. His death, dockside, waiting for the dawn, is very poignant. And Sarah Polley's evolution from everyday nurse to kick-ass heroine is handled quite realistically. In this movie stereotypes become real characters and the actors breathe life into each and every role.

The pre-title sequence of *Dawn of the Dead* is simply classic and perhaps might represent modern horror's finest moment. In this roughly 10-minute sequence, Sarah Polley leaves the hospital after dealing with several emergency patients who have been admitted with bite wounds. Going home to her husband, this turns out to be their "date" night and they quickly make it into the transparent shower and

engage in passionate lovemaking. Soon nestled in their bed, the husband sees his door open with the motionless figure of a young girl, a child, simply standing near the edge of the room. Wide-eyed and out of sorts, the husband goes over to speak to the intruding female, when in fierce aggression the child quickly bites the husband in his neck, severing flesh and arteries with blood gushing. The nurse attends to her husband and tries to phone 911, but he dies momentarily from the loss of blood, with the zombie child in hot pursuit, who flings the rag doll Polley against the wall. She quickly recovers and bolts herself in her bathroom; the door is smashed down by the predator who grabs Polley's bare legs and feet as she squeezes out of the window onto her lawn. Racing for her car, she encounters both zombies and neighbors armed with rifles, but she speeds off down the street. Many neighborhood homes are under barrage and some are even going up in flames. Aerial views (something the original production could never afford) show her car from the air speeding down the highways as buildings burn, some explode, and cars seem to crash into ditches all around her. She finally is forced off the road and cruises down an embankment where she hits a tree and is soon discovered by the Ving Rhames character. But for mere velocity of horror and action, with marvelous cinematography accenting all the proper notes, this pre-title sequence is masterfully executed, and while it may be one of the stellar sequences in the entire movie, what follows afterwards is consistently effective.

As the survivors barricade themselves inside the mall and make their way up to the roof to paint rescue signs for helicopters flying overhead to see, Ving Rhames discovers that one other survivor, isolated and alone, is on his rooftop (Andy's Gun Shop) unable to reach the other survivors by nature of the fact that armies of zombies are milling throughout the streets below. Using marker boards to communicate, Rhames and Andy communicate via short messages and even play games (such as chess) to while away the hours. One of the most clever games they play is "shoot the celebrity" when they identify zombies who resemble celebrities—such as Burt Reynolds and Jay Leno—and Andy, a pot shot, spills their brains on cement below. Touches such as these elevate the movie above the work of similar movies and make it stand apart from the original. The supplemental materials even include a video "found" depicting Andy's final days but told from his point of view. A very nice touch.

Unlike Romero's zombies who methodically and slowly roamed throughout the mall, the zombies in Snyder's *Dawn of the Dead* are rabid, quick moving and deadly. They lack the characterizations of the almost comical Romero walking corpses, but they substitute that loss with ferocious horror (becoming closer in execution to Romero's underground zombies from *Day of the Dead*). The Unrated Director's cut is the version to see, and with all the extras featuring a superior Dolby 5.1 soundtrack, *Dawn of the Dawn* be-gins to restore hope for the future of modern horror cinema. To put it another way, I can't wait to see this one again.

It has just been announced that *Dawn of the Dead* will have a sequel filmed within the year. Not, not a remake of *Day of the Dead*, but an original sequel. How curious!

I Married a Monster from Outer Space
Movie: 3.0; Disc: 3.0
[Paramount Home Video]

Everyone has always, to my way of thinking, over-praised Gene Fowler, Jr.'s eccentric *I Married a Monster from Outer Space*. For a B production, it always seems to be too classy when compared to its peers (even Gene Fowler's own *I Was a Teenage Werewolf*) and thus gained a reputation as being a cut above. However, when compared to those superior films *I Married a Monster from Outer Space* imitated, well, the film pales in comparison. Let me explain exactly what I mean.

Basically, *I Married a Monster from Outer Space* mimics superior loss of identity aliens-look-just-like-us movies such as *Enemy from Space* and, of course, *Invasion of the Body Snatchers*. We have the alien who possesses the body of Tom Tyron and his best buddy, but also possesses most of the police force of the town, and many other citizens. Borrowing the technique from *It Came from Outer Space*, the aliens take possession from a subjective camera point of view by releasing cosmic fog that permeates and enshrouds unwilling victims. Instead of marks or incisions on the back of people's necks, we have the inner alien shining brightly through during electrical storms, mostly during moments of pounding thunder and flickering lightning. However, Gene Fowler, Jr.'s execution is not nearly as creative as these other productions.

When we are shown the cleverly crafted monsters, the movie shines, as this is less psychological horror but more monsters from space. The climactic battle in the woods, with the dogs released to attack the aliens, becomes perhaps the film's outstanding sequence, and when the aliens are mortally wounded, turning to putrid slime via stop-motion photography, the film resembles the classy *Fiend Without a Face*.

The film's small budget becomes painfully apparent in the representation of the alien rocket ship that somehow lies hidden in the thick wooded brush (and it is never clearly seen from top to bottom), just a hop and skip from the neighborhood road. The shot of the ship's interior where the real humans are monitored and suspended from eerie mechanical hanging devices is very effective, but the film's suburban American landscape seems to be hiding the need for more expansive sets (William Cameron Menzies did wonders with the similarly themed *Invaders from Mars* with an invasion occurring in Jimmy Hunt's backyard).

However, the film's strength tries to be the sensitive characterizations of the just-married Tom Tryon and Gloria Talbott, and this may very well be Talbott's finest performance. She plays the sensitive wife who is a sexually frustrated woman who tries to light a sexual spark in Tryon's trousers, yet fails. Tryon is less successful, relying on his short-sleeved and gawky exposed arms to convey the sense that he is a stranger in his own human body. Tryon's arms are very long and lanky, and the manner in which he awkwardly holds himself tries to convey the obvious fact that he is a stranger in a strange skin. But his verbal delivery of lines, his facial reactions and expressions and his too obvious sense that he is in fact an alien compromise the performance by making it too "dude's an alien!" obvious.

In spite of the flaws, *I Married a Monster from Outer Space*, while it suffers in comparison to the films that inspired it, still comes off as moody, gripping and spooky and it is a solid sci-fi horror entry. Other than the deep contrasted widescreen print that is enhanced for 16:9 monitors, no extras are included.

John Carpenter's The Thing [Special Edition]
Movie: 3.5; Disc: 3.5
[Universal Home Video]

John Carpenter has to be one of the luckiest people in Hollywood. By adding a dose of creativity and artistic vision to the exploitative *Halloween*, he created a special niche for himself as one of the true independents of the last 30 years. While most of his movies are wonderful B productions, his is not a talent that is particularly eccentric nor visionary. Journeyman horror director describes him perfectly. However, twice in his career he created movies of remarkable vision—first independently with *Halloween* and then in 1982 with the mainstream Hollywood Universal production of the remark of *The Thing*. I consider both movies to be modern horror classics and the finest example of Carpenter's cinematic oeuvre.

I loved John Carpenter's *The Thing* back in 1982 and, not surprisingly, the film holds up and remains one of the best examples of modern horror, even with its special makeup effects focus. While Rob Bottin's grotesque H.P. Lovecraftian alien designs are no longer state of the art, they still are powerful monster images that both attract our attention and repulse us, at the same time. The major weakness of the production, the lack of personality in the ensemble cast, seems less of a flaw today (even when compared to Howard Hawks' ensemble cast from the original *The Thing*, always praised for its sparkling use of overlapping dialogue that brings that cast to vibrant life). Perhaps Wilford Brimley's freak-out sequence where he fires his pistol with abandonment screaming through clenched jaws, "I will *kiiiillllll* you!!!!" does go over the top. But the performances, for the most part, are appropriate and enthralling. Remember, these are military men facing the beginning of a harsh winter alone and cut off from civilization—in Antarctica. So they spend time whiling away the hours roller-skating, listening to music, drinking and working. These aren't necessarily dull men, but they are men dulled by their circumstances and environment.

But what a masterful job Carpenter creates with the cinematography of Dean Cundey and the subtlety of Ennio Marricone's musical score (which is compromised by additional music cues created by John Carpenter himself, who usually scores his own productions). We have the camera snake, at a low level, around all the endless mazes of corridors and supply rooms and kennels. In the masterful open-ing sequence, a helicopter of Norwegians tracking a lone dog through the snow trying to shoot the animal to death. After the copter explodes and one lone gunman pursues the dog through the American camp, the Norwegian is shot in the head for his dangerous and off-aim shooting. In these early sequences the dog is subtly followed as he interacts with the men at the camp, entering the room of one man in eerie silhouette, signaling this is a pivotal moment. The first slam-bang sequence soon follows as this wolfish dog is placed, finally, in the kennel where he is immediately snarled and hissed at by the other dogs. Soon the alien inside is released as the dog's head splits open and the alien presence attempts to absorb the other dogs before it is incinerated by the now alert military personnel.

And the movie's best sequence, the blood serum test to check who

treme claustrophobia with subtle sequences that chill the bone without special effects or gore. The tracking sequence following the alien dog throughout the camp is one such sequence. Another is the investigation of the Norwegian camp and finding their outpost where they melted the alien saucer and dug out the frozen monster. Some of these sequences are created on video and others occur with just musical accompaniment without dialogue. In another sequence we have the men bumping into one another and sounding alarms, panicking over what they think they see and hear. Carpenter's di-rectorial talent is readily seen in such sequences.

The Collector's Edi-tion features a re-mastered Dolby 5.1 Surround print, anamorphic and pristine. The only flaw is that the medium shots that show people sometimes have a video double edge to their outlines. This is slightly annoying but isn't a major flaw. This use to be a flaw in older DVD mastering, but not so much recently. But for $15 who can complain! Extras include the usual audio commentary, a newly produced (and quite good) 80-minute documentary about the production of the film, outtakes and work-in-progress

is still human and who is alien, remains one of horror cinema's finest moments. With most of the men tied to their chairs with Kurt Russell dipping his hot wire into the petrie dish filled with each individual's blood, the suspense is intense. This sequence would be doomed to failure if it wasn't for the audience concern for Carpenter's ensemble cast and each individual's characterization. And when the least likely candidate is revealed to be the alien in human clothing, with many men still tied up and Kurt Russell's flame-thrower unable to produce a flame, everyone in the house is screaming.

Also as effective is the sequence where the doctor uses a defibrillator to revive another of the men at camp and his arms crash through the man's chest as monstrous jaws hack his hands off at the wrist. Soon the man's human head rips itself from the torso and transforms into an alien spider with the man's head prancing across the floor. Such sequences constantly bombard the movie viewer and keep the production in scare mode eternally.

But besides the big scares, Carpenter permeates his production with foreboding isolation and ex- special effects work and sequences that never made it into the final cut of the film. The extras are worth the price of admission. But it is gratifying that John Carpenter's *The Thing* still holds up well and remains one of the defining moments in 1980s horror cinema.

Creature from the Black Lagoon (1954)
Revenge of the Creature (1955)
The Creature Walks Among Us (1956)
The Legacy Collection
Movies: *Black Lagoon* 3.0;
Revenge: 2.0;
Walks: 2.5; Disc: 3.5
[Universal Home Video]

Twenty-plus years after the onslaught of the original Universal beasties of the 1930s, the studio's movie monster mythology returned with a vengeance with the Gill Man, the signature monster of the baby boomer generation, the last great Universal monster. Within a period of three years, Universal produced three movies starring the Gill Man, movies that never quite rose up artistically to the level of the monster that was featured in all of them. But nonetheless, the Black Lagoon trilogy remains a pivotal movie series that lingers 50 years later.

Without doubt, the original entry, *Creature from the Black Lagoon*, is the pick of the litter, and although quite pedestrian in execution, it still manages to both fascinate and terrify. Director Jack Arnold, whose *It Came from Outer Space* is much more stylishly and eerily directed, and whose latter film *The Incredible Shrinking Man* is considered his masterpiece, perhaps went to his grave knowing *Creature from the Black Lagoon* would be his most remembered production. Arnold spent most of his directorial time working with the land crew and the land-based sequences, while another crew worked on the underwater shots. The film is most noteworthy for those shimmering, sharp underwater sequences that depict the long and leggy Julia Adams, in her white swim suit, almost operatically swimming on or near the surface of the water while the Gill Man silently (yet intensely) watches her, swimming almost in synch with her, further underneath the surface. Filmed almost as a ritualistic mating water ballet, the film never gets better than these scenes. The wavering light shining through the water sequence when Adams treads water, her legs and feet dangling within inches of the creature's playful grope, her feet shaking off the tickling sensation she feels when the Gill Man is inches away from her toes, remains an iconic moment in horror cinema. Other sequences near the end of the movie, showing how the Gill Man swims to an underwater grotto, which somehow leads to the beach area, are actually as scary as the movie ever becomes. The Gill Man often suddenly appears or jumps out of the water, hopping aboard the boat, immediately plunging back into the water with his victim dead or Julia Adams in his arms. But perhaps the most haunting creature shots are when the beast is confined to a partially underwater bamboo cage, the Gill Man's head exposed above the water, his mouth open and gasping for air. Somehow those haunting quiet scenes, rare as they are, seem to imbue a rubber-like suit with spirit and life.

Even though *Creature from the Black Lagoon* is a B movie, Universal Pictures created B+ productions unlike any other studio and it is because of Jack Arnold's serious approach that the movie is not more fun in the sense the movie was so bad it was outrageous fun. The movie meanders at its own leisurely pace, and while things never get quite boring, the movie features few pinnacles that linger decades later. The two male stars, the dedicated scientist played by Richard Carlson vs. the entrepreneur played by Richard Denning, create romantic friction for Julia Adams. But somehow Nestor Naiva's crusty old seaman almost manages to steal the show. An adequate movie featuring a classic monster is perhaps the best way to sum up the production. Extras include audio commentary, theatrical trailer, production photographs and a wonderful documentary of the entire series containing interviews with some of the surviving cast and crew.

Revenge of the Creature followed one year later in 1955, and this time the star was perennial 1950s hero John Agar looking robust and handsome as a scientific observer. Lori Nelson, more squat and less

CREATURE FROM THE BLACK LAGOON
THE LEGACY COLLECTION

looks like a prefab costume. For instance, the constant air bubbles coming from the Gill Man's head in the sequel become distracting, making the monster appear to be a scuba driver in latex. The way the arms fit into the shoulders makes the Gill Man appear too patchwork. And while the underwater sequences were filled with suspense and tension in the original, acquiring a dreamlike reality that becomes quite haunting, here the underwater tank sequences appear to be a dull travelogue of sea life. Besides the strong presence of John Agar, this Gill Man entry has very little to offer, and it most definitely becomes dull during its brief 80-minute running time. Extras include audio commentary (including Lori Nelson) and theatrical trailer. When people speak about how sequels pale when compared to the original, *Revenge of the Creature* is the perfect example. A programmer without inspiration is sad indeed.

The final Gill Man entry, released one year later in 1956, was a step above the quality of *Revenge of the Creature*. At least in *The Creature Walks Among Us* a premise existed beyond "let's capture and observe this missing link to man." With an all-star cast of horror-based performers, eccentric scientist Jeff Morrow wishes to operate on the Gill

leggy than Julia Adams, plays the heroine, also a scientist, who teams up with Agar. Jack Arnold returns as director, but unfortunately, this entry is by far the worst of the series. With nary a thread of plot and with most of the action occurring at Florida's Marineland, the menacing Gill Man seems powerless and almost fragile. In a few sequences near the movie's end he does cause a commotion, but these sequences are few and far between. Strange how the actors who played the Gill Man never received onscreen credit. Only in their media convention moneymaking afterlife did they rear their heads above water and muck to make tidy profits from their fans. Also the suit designed for this first sequel pales when compared to the original suit that

Man to beat evolutionary scientists and have the creature become land based and more human. On the other hand we have sensitive scientist Rex Reason argue that evolution must be allowed to take its course, that human interference will never work. Along for the voyage of discovery is another leggy beauty, Leigh Snowden, who portrays Morrow's dissatisfied wife who starts to fall for Rex Reason, and, of course, the evolving Gill Man also has eyes for the beauty. For the first 40 minutes or so, the Gill Man is as we expect him to be, lurking beneath the Amazon waters eluding capture from the invading humans. The sequences showing his capture and subsequent burning (resulting in Morrow getting his wish to operate, to force the Gill Man to now breathe using his lungs and no longer his gills) are well photographed and gripping. However, the second half of the movie occurs with the reconstructed creature, looking far more human, being contained and observed at Morrow's scientific plantation. In a few clever sequences, the audience can literally feel the Gill Man's isolation at longingly looking out at the sea, desiring to return to his beloved water, only to realize that he can no longer breathe under water and that he is, literally, neither fish nor fowl. His escape and psychopathic outrage at the film's conclusion is quite exciting and well paced. Of course Jeff Morrow gets thrown to his death, literally being held over the Gill Man's shoulders, and the audience loves to see the cruel scientist get his just reward. At least this third entry attempts to further the concept introduced in the first production and try to say something new about the last great Universal monster. Still, *The Creature Walks Among Us* is adequate at best and perhaps should be remembered for the dueling scientists and a sensitive performance by Don Megowan as the redesigned creature. Extras include audio commentary and a theatrical trailer.

To be honest, this Legacy box set from Universal is a treat and should be purchased by every Universal Monster fan. However, while most of the other box sets contain five features, this box set only contains three. Wouldn't it have been clever to contain both 2-D and 3-D versions of *Creature from the Black Lagoon* and *Revenge of the Creature*, complete with two or three pairs of 3-D glasses? In this way the Creature Legacy box would have contained five features as well. Universal did itself proud!

Eyes Without A Face
Movie: 4.0; Disc: 3.5
[Criterion Collection]

Amazing that more "left of the dial" horror classics are not being released by Criterion, for their presentation of *Fiend Without a Face* was superb and remains the finest looking remastered 1950s science fiction horror film on DVD. A series of Richard Gordon B productions are also forthcoming from Criterion. But at last one of my favorite horror films ever, Georges Franju's *Eyes Without a Face*, is finally released to DVD (its Image release on Laserdisc a decade ago was essential viewing) and it has never looked better. Totally remastered (both picture and sound), the movie now features inky blacks with nuances of gray, and the odd, quirky musical score by Maurice Jarre just shimmers.

Many of us first encountered *Eyes Without a Face* in its butchered American re-edited version, 1963's *The Horror Chamber of Dr. Faustus*, the other half of the double-bill with *The Manster*. But that bastardized version is nothing like seeing the original French Franju version. The movie's stark black and white photography by Eugen Schufftan (aka Shuftan) is among the eeriest ever concocted for a horror film classic, showcasing naked corpses in trench coats being dumped into a river, dank kennels with raging dogs in cages, the no-frills operating room, the cold police station, the darkly lit morgue and the gloomy mausoleum, each establishing set pieces of morbid and depressed horror. *Eyes Without a Face* is not a black and white movie; it is best described as black and gray.

The three performances that tantalize are the wonderful Pierre Brasseur as Dr. Genessier, Alida Valli as his assistant Louise and Edith Scob as Genessier's daughter Christiane. Brasseur is perhaps the horror genre's most unique mad doctor simply because he underplays the role to absolute perfection. His frozen face and hollow eyes are sublime when he is called to the morgue and asked to identify his daughter, which he does (even though the corpse belongs to that of his victim, *not* his own daughter). And when the actual father of the victim pleads with Genessier with tear-filled eyes to confirm the corpse was the doctor's daughter, Genessier coldly accuses the desperate man of trying to squeeze comfort from him when it is his own daughter who is dead, cold on the slab. Such an icy demeanor only accentuates the internal evil this doctor projects, a doctor who is sacrificing young victims to attempt to restore his daughter's ravished face, a face destroyed in an auto accident caused by Genessier himself. Creating a counterpart to the over-the-top mad doc played by a Colin Clive or a Bela Lugosi, Pierre Brasseur is always coolly calculating and all his rage and pain is internal, silently held in check. It's a masterful performance.

Alida Valli, soon to be known a generation later for her appearances in Italian horror movies, is interesting in an almost silent role as assistant (her face also reconstructed... a scar on her neck hidden by necklaces) to Genessier (it is always apparent she loves the doctor and will do anything for him) who silently waits unseen in cars on crowded Paris streets, attempting to find the right young girl with the

proper facial features to become the latest medical guinea pig. In other sequences she becomes almost like a mother to the disturbed Christiane, comforting the girl and giving her strength and faith that her father will be able to restore her face. Valli's is a supporting role, but it is one that lingers.

But perhaps the most interesting performance is that of Edith Scob as the hauntingly beautiful Christiane, the girl who wears an ivory white face mask that only reveals her hair and eyes, making her face as rigid yet as beautiful as any statue crafted by any Italian artist. Christiane is often viewed curled up in a fetal position on the couch. Her wide, sad eyes are a mirror to her soul, revealing a young woman lost in hopelessness. Even after her face is restored and the mask is gone, her actual facial features do not appear much different than when she was wearing the mask, but her short-term hope is lost as her face slowly deteriorates, captured in a series of still photographs shot over the course of almost one week. Earlier, from a subjective focus, the audience caught a blurred shot of Christiane's mask-less face as she stared at the face of the victim-to-be lying helpless on the operating table. Christiane's depression is caused by the fact that even if the operation is successful, her success means the disfigurement or even death of an innocent girl, much like herself. At the movie's climax she releases the wild dogs, who attack and maul the face of the unsuspecting Dr. Genessier, and the doves, whose white presence in the dark night is more an image of beauty on which to end the film rather than a logical plot resolution. *Eyes Without a Face* ends on such a note of quiet, intense beauty, allowing such imagery to create a dramatic conclusion.

Eyes Without a Face lies in my top-25 horror film favorites, and this wonderful Criterion Collection DVD presents the film to absolute perfection. The wonderful liner notes and analysis by David Kalat and Patrick McGrath add immeasurably to the enjoyment of the film, and on-disc extras include interviews with the movie's screenwriters and director (appearing on what appears to be a foreign version of a creature feature TV presentation), still and poster gallery and trailers. Most disturbing is the inclusion of the 1949 documentary short *Blood of the Beasts*, which is an award-winning glimpse of the everyday work of those men who work in the Paris slaughterhouses killing, gutting horses, cows, sheep in such a non-chalant manner (cigarettes dangle from their mouths as they perform their daily duties by rote, without emotion). To my eyes, this short is the most disturbing movie I ever witnessed and my honest advice to anyone buying the disc is a simple one: Do not watch it! Or be prepared to become a vegetarian!

Eyes Without a Face is a masterpiece presented here in a masterful way. For me it might very well be my favorite DVD of 2004. It is a movie to be discovered and enjoyed. In 1959 Hammer was at its artistic peak. *Eyes Without A Face* demonstrates what France was creating at the same time.

The Mummy (1932)
The Mummy's Hand (1940)
The Mummy's Tomb (1942)
The Mummy's Ghost (1944)
The Mummy's Curse (1944)
The Legacy Collection
Movies: *Mummy:* 3.5; *Hand:* 3.0; *Tomb:* 2.0; *Ghost:* 2.5; *Curse:* 2.5; Disc: 3.5
[Universal Home Video]

Universal's Mummy series, actually one stand-alone production and an unrelated series of sequels, is one of the more entertaining B series ever produced, horror or otherwise. First of all, the original *The Mummy* features one of icon Boris Karloff's best performances and is a classic of the horror cinema. The sequels, starring Tom Tyler and then Lon Chaney, Jr., are silly and juvenile, but they are also atmospheric, fast-paced, beautifully dressed and photographed for low budget productions, effectively acted—and most of all—entertaining.

Universal's classic *The Mummy*, similar in plot execution to the studio's earlier hit *Dracula*, is one of the hallmarks of horror cinema. Director Karl Freund, always the classically trained cinematographer, makes *The Mummy* perhaps the most visually elaborate and subtle of any Universal horror classic. Just look at the beautifully rendered reanimation sequence where Bramwell Fletcher reads from the Scroll of Thoth and the all-so-slow crumbling hand of Karloff's extends to grasp the parchment, as Fletcher abruptly turns and laughs hysterically at the presence of an unseen mummy walking away. How rare to stage such a pivotal sequence only showing the mummy's hand and not its entire body, but Fletcher's maniacal laughter says it all. Freund's control of the camera shines in those sequences where we dive into the pool of the past where, with quick montages, Freund depicts the ill-fated love affair between Imhotep and his Princess.

Besides his Frankenstein portrayals, Boris Karloff's Imhotep is perhaps his shining achievement, subtly underplaying body movements and delivery of dialogue. As Ardath Bey, the degree of mummification of his face changing from corpse-like to almost human, Karloff moves as though a sudden jerk would reduce him to crumbling ash, and his dialogue is delivered, sometimes forcefully, as though his body were drained of every ounce of energy and speaking aloud becomes a deliberate effort. Karloff, who is frequently accused of overacting, here proves Ardath Bey an utter triumph by deliberately underplaying every sequence. Zita Johann, wearing a very skimpy costume by movie's end (I wonder if the censors would have allowed the costume if Johann's breasts had been larger), submits a quite eccentric performance, one of the better female leads of any Universal production by virtue of the fact that Johann has the opportunity to create a well-defined character, one who has lived through the ages via reincarnation. As her memory is jogged and she begins to remember her past lives and ultimately accepts the power of Egyptian god Isis, Johann turns from typical horror heroine to a rather morbidly developed character of depth.

And what ultimately makes *The Mummy* a unique horror masterpiece is the fact that the script blends elements of a corpse rising from the dead with a romantic reincarnation tale of love surviving beyond mortal flesh for 3,700 years. Two years earlier Universal tried to deliver the same premise with *Dracula*, but *The Mummy* delivers the goods.

Eight years later Universal revisited the soon-to-be franchise by dropping Imhotep and creating a new character, Kharis, to become the new franchise Mummy, one who would remain trapped in his decaying bandages and stalk those intruders who insensitively entered sacred Egyptian burial tombs. No human form Ardath Bey here… the Mummy would remain the monstrous mummy, crippled and dragging one leg behind yet still managing to sneak up upon fallen, cowering victims. Universal's *The Mummy's Hand*, the only one featuring Western/serial star Tom Tyler as Kharis, is the best of all the sequels, even though stars Wallace Ford and Dick Foran seem to be vying for Universal's top spot comedy team with their wise-cracking shenanigans. Tom Tyler has the monstrous Mummy look and movement down pat, aided by the optical effects of blacking out his eyes, making him appear more monstrous and ungodly. The sequences utilizing standing sets from a James Whale movie add immeasurably to the Egyptian décor. When Kharis saunters across a wide set decorated with Egyptian temple and huge statues, it takes him forever to move, but the visuals behind him hold the audience's attention. Also the introduction of Eduardo Ciannelli as the High Priest of Karnak and George Zucco as his

replacement create both mythos and memorable villains, especially Zucco, who manages to survive throughout most of the movie. The fact is that *The Mummy's Hand* is a B production, but a B production with a budget, expensive-looking sets and ceremonial steps, allowing the production a visual depth lost on the remainder of the sequels. And Tyler's performance as the Mummy is truly terrifying, setting the standard for Lon Chaney to carry on.

In 1942 Lon Chaney, Jr. was unrecognizable as Kharis in *The Mummy's Tomb*, perhaps the worst

of the entire Kharis series. First of all, the movie only runs one hour yet almost one quarter is devoted to flashback footage of what happened in the past two movies. Also, the characters of Dick Foran and Wallace Ford return, in pathetic age make-ups that look ridiculous. By the end of the movie, both heroes from the previous entry are dead, the victims of Kharis. This is very similar as to what happened at the beginning of *Alien 3* where we learn that Newt and other survivors from *Aliens* have not survived. It's a very downer way of initiating a new entry in a franchise series.

And poor Lon Chaney, Jr.! For years fans disputed the fact that Chaney, Jr. even appeared under the mummy makeup, and while now most people accept the fact that Lon Chaney, Jr. allowed himself to become little more than a stuntman, submitting a performance on the level of a Ben Chapman, the makeup does whatever it can to undermine Chaney, Jr.'s performance. First of all, as photographed, Chaney appears to be short and fairly rotund, not ever the imposing figure that Tom Tyler was. Also, one of his eyes has been gauzed over and his face is frozen under the makeup, so he cannot even emote using facial expressions. For me this is the worst makeup, physical appearance and acting ever executed in a Universal Mummy movie.

Now aged and palsied, George Zucco passes the message of the nine tana leaves to young and handsome high priest Turhan Bey, whose performance is creepy and effective, as he becomes caretaker of the local cemetery. His appearances alone and with Kharis become the high point of the movie, but once again the movie becomes silly in the manner in which the crippled Mummy (one frozen arm and a crippled leg which he drags behind him) always manages to creep up upon his unfortunate victim and literally throttle him with one decaying hand. However, the flaming inferno ending does manage to drum up some suspense, so the film is not without some merit.

In 1943 Kharis and Lon Chaney, Jr. return in the slightly improved *The Mummy's Ghost* where George Zucco hands the tana leaves over to long and lanky John Carradine, another sexual predator High Priest of Karnak who only wants to bed the heroine by making both himself and her immortal. It is only at times like these that Kharis, in a jealous rage, has to ultimately murder his caretaker High Priest and thus destroy his means of surviving.

However, the makeup for *The Mummy's Ghost* is much more effective and expressive than the makeup for *The Mummy's Tomb*, and the visage of Chaney, Jr. is easily recognized. As he squints and grimaces, the facial makeup is less rubbery and nuances of expression are easily accomplished by the actor within the bandages. In this production we have no flashbacks for, in one sequence, a college professor shares the 30-year history in his classroom in two minutes. The most praiseworthy addition is not necessarily the performance by Ramsey Ames as the heroine (she is rather lackluster and pretty in an odd sense) but the manner in which the audience is told that she is the reincarnation of the Princess Ananka by the ever-increasing white streak in her hair. By the time Carradine has her tied down in his railroad shack and is ready to inject her with the herbs to make her immortal, her hair is all white. When Kharis carries her beneath the swamp water, not only is her hair white, but her face has become mummified and wrinkled. This concept, to be followed in the final entry, is rather interesting and disturbing. And it picks up on the dominant reincarnation theme in Karloff's original. This third sequel has established the formula. We have invaders of ancient Egyptian tombs who need to be punished by High Priests of the Egyptian gods. The mythology that three tana leaves keep Kharis' heart beating, nine give him mobility, is entrusted to various high priests who pass on the motive and means of revenge to younger acolytes. Generally the right-minded high priests live on the outskirts of small-town America, gleefully carrying out their ritualistic murder. However, good old lust intervenes as the high priest gets the hots for the beautiful young heroine and promises her immortality for a roll in the sack. This makes Kharis angry (he who was tortured, has his tongue cut out and is buried alive for daring to love the wrong woman) and the movie ends up with the high priest dead and Kharis dead. Sorta.

But all this slightly changes in the final entry, 1944's *The Mummy's Curse*, whose location of Mapletown has been changed to the Louisiana Bayou where, as one local declares, the devil's alive and he's dancing with the Mummy. It seems the swamp where Kharis took his Princess Ananka at the conclusion of *The Mummy's Ghost* floated way, way down south. In the film's best sequence, heroine Virginia Christine slowly emerges from the sun-baked clay and pulls herself out of her burial bog to slowly and quite eerily walk to a nearby pond where she can wash the clay, dirt and age off. Emerging from the swampy earth mummified, a little water changes her into a beautiful young woman.

The Cajun plotline revolves around an engineer drying the swampland using locals for his labor force, but the locals are fearful of people who entered the swamp alive but were later found dead. Just like the usual gang of Universal ensemble players, these locals are afraid of the Mummy mythos and do not wish to

be a victim of Kharis (unfortunately, to fill out the hour running time, we again feature flashback footage from *The Mummy's Hand* showing Tom Tyler as Kharis and sequences filmed for the 1932 *The Mummy* featuring Boris Karloff as Imhotep). This time the most nondescript high priest, Peter Coe, has an ally in local Cajun Martin Kosleck who is the hit man for seemingly above-the-board Coe and does his dirty work. That is until the duo reanimates the long dormant Kharis, now also miraculously rescued from the swamp waters and ready to become a vehicle for revenge. The makeup this time is quite detailed and monstrous and Lon Chaney's features are once again easily recognized. However, once he slurps the tana juice, the rubbery mask quality of his facial makeup tends to undermine the effect. Sometimes the photographer makes Kharis appear like a candidate for a Sideshow Toy doll, while at other times the makeup is not as effective and Kharis is not as carefully photographed (in one sequence his dangling bandages near his feet look like trousers that can be put on and off). And of course Kharis is always played with one crippled arm and leg, but he somehow gets the jump on his victims. In one effective sequence the caretaker comes upon the unsuspecting Coe and Kosleck, and while Coe is soft-talking the angry caretaker, we have intercuts of an angered Kharis all so slowly approaching. It takes two or three intercuts before the Mummy sneaks up, without making any noise, and manages to get his one good hand around the victim's neck. But this is the fun of these B features that Universal did so well.

Extras on this Legacy box set are features that appeared originally on the individual releases of each feature. We have a wonderful documentary, *Mummy Dearest: A Horror Tradition Unearthed*, hosted by David J. Skal. We have Paul Jensen's insightful audio commentary for the original *The Mummy*. We have a photo/poster gallery included. And lastly, we have trailers of all five films. Compared to the Frankenstein, Wolf Man and Dracula series of the 1930s and 1940s, the Mummy series, even though quite atmospheric, moody and featuring a fabulous monster, comes in next to last place (with last place reserved for the Invisible Man series). The features end up being a little too similar with too much recap or flashback footage used to fill up time. However, these movies (especially the Karloff original and the first sequel with Tom Tyler) deserve a special niche in horror film history, and this magnificent box set is a fitting tribute to Universal's horror factory.

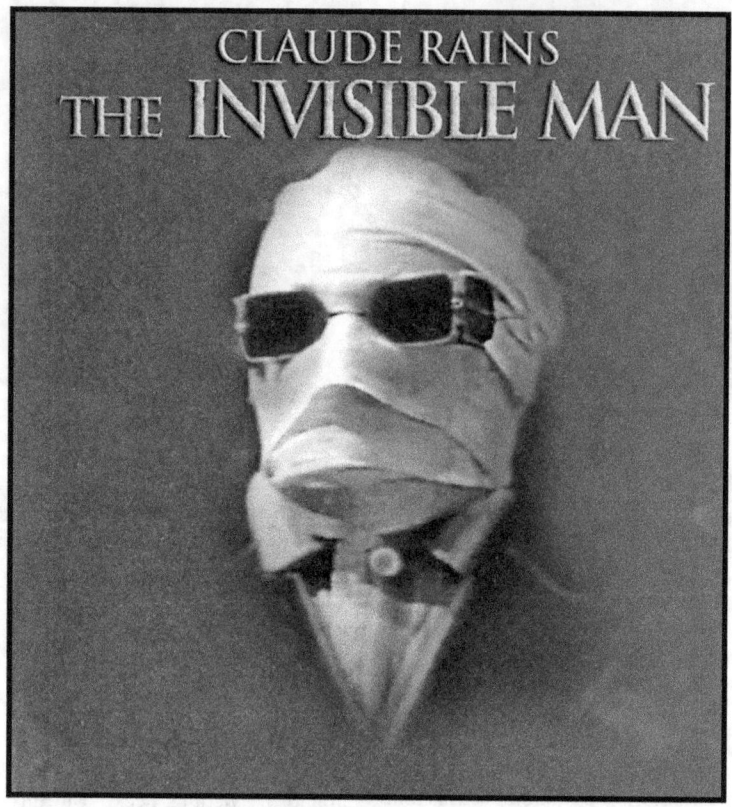

The Invisible Man (1933)
The Invisible Man Returns (1940)
The Invisible Man's Revenge (1944)
The Invisible Woman (1944)
The Invisible Agent (1942)
The Legacy Collection
Movies: *Invisible Man*: 3.0; *Returns*: 2.5; *Revenge*: 2.5; *Woman* 2.0; *Agent*: 2.0;
Disc: 3.5
[Universal Home Video]

Let the truth be known! James Whale and Terence Fisher are my two favorite horror film directors and I love *Frankenstein*, *Bride of Frankenstein*, and *The Old Dark House*. However, *The Invisible Man*, for me, is the Universal clunker and the absolute worst of 1930s horror. There, I said it.

James Whale's *The Invisible Man* still warrants three stars and is a good film, but it is also a distressingly frustrating and ultimately disappointing classic. For once I find the contradiction in tone between the snowy entrance of Jack Griffin wrapped in gauze booking a room at the inn—the sequence played for true mystery and horror—and latter sequences of an over-the-top maniac dancing in his shirt tops chasing Keystone cops around the room. The blending of horror and humor works to maximum satisfaction in *Bride of Frankenstein* and *The Old Dark House*, but in *The Invisible Man* it seems both grating and silly.

First, what works in the movie is the photography, performances by the leads (Claude Rains, Una O'Connor, Gloria Stuart and William Harrigan) and Whale's direction in those sequences that create a dank and ominous mood. I admit my bias is more toward horror than science fiction, and while John P. Fulton's special effects are exceptional for the time, another flaw of the movie is Whale's focusing too heavily on the silly effects that appear very dated today. The best special effect in the movie is Claude Rains' heavily made up visage, his white bandaged face and chin, his darkened glasses and his gloved hands, all shot in intense close-up, making Jack Griffin's presence impossible to ignore. And Rains' line readings, his dialogue bellowing from a small body, create a performance based upon voice and bandages, and it is a dynamite iconic performance in an at best good vehicle. The sequences at the inn with Griffin demanding to be left alone to finish his work with the Cockney supporting players responding with suspicion and fear peaks the dramatic tension in the first quarter of the movie. Not until Griffin invades the home of Dr. Kemp (William Harrigan) and literally forces the sniveling scientist to become his

brother in arms (to conquer the world and lead its dominions) does the drama regenerate to that intensity again. In one tense sequence Kemp calls the police, but a car carrying love interest Flora (Gloria Stuart) and Dr. Cranley (Henry Travers) first pulls up in plain sight of Griffin. Griffin immediately accuses Kemp of calling the police and betraying him, creating a tension that builds until Griffin escapes through the hands-held police cordon. Threatening to kill Kemp 10 o'clock the next night, Griffin finds the disguised Kemp alone in his getaway car and cold-bloodedly sends his former colleague and his vehicle off a cliff (Griffin at first detailing all the pain and bodily damage Kemp will sustain before his neck is broken), the car exploding midway down the embankment.

Surprisingly, the film's pacing is lethargic and the plot spends too much time on upset citizenry and snoopy police stalking the wilderness for their invisible man. The film's tone is goofy, quaint and comical when the film needs to be suspenseful, spooky and dark. While James Whale's direction in key scenes is spot on, in many others, he seems to miss his mark and allows tedium and mediocrity to rule. Fortunately supporting players E.E. Clive and Una O'Connor, presented for their comic shenanigans, are wonderfully drawn because their humorous antics are always laced with dread, fear and horror, not comedy for its own sake.

For me, *The Invisible Man* is the most disappointing of all 1930s horror classics, and a boxed DVD set based upon the spawn of this initial thriller is bound to disappoint.

For instance, Universal's direct sequel, *The Invisible Man Returns*, is most remembered for its wonderfully green one-sheet poster rather than for the production itself. Even with a cast comprised of Cedric Hardwicke, Nan Gray, Vincent Price and Cecil Kellaway, under Joe May's direction, *The Invisible Man Returns* is predictable. Geoffrey (Vincent Price), accused of murdering his brother, awaits execution while seedy and shifty-eyed cousin Cobb (Cedric Hardwicke) makes a phone call and sadly announces he can do nothing to stay the execution, even though he has friends in high places. Cobb's guilt is early telegraphed, and when Frank Griffin, brother to the original movie's Jack Griffin, goes to visit the death row prisoner hours before his execution, and Geoffrey disappears with only a pile of his clothes left behind in the jail cell, audiences know exactly what has happened. Geoffrey, now invisible, must solve his brother's murder to clear himself before the invisibility drug, now called duocane, makes him insane as it did his brother Jack. Even amid the interesting mining locale with high hill tracks, the suspense is minimal, performances are adequate and the direction lethargic. The gimmick of invisibility created by John Fulton may have fascinated at the time, but today, the shirt and trousers dancing playfully about or a suspended newspaper floating in air is not a special effect for all time (however Cecil Kellaway's smoking a cigar, blowing smoke, and seeing the outline of Geoffrey and lurching for him *is*; another excellent

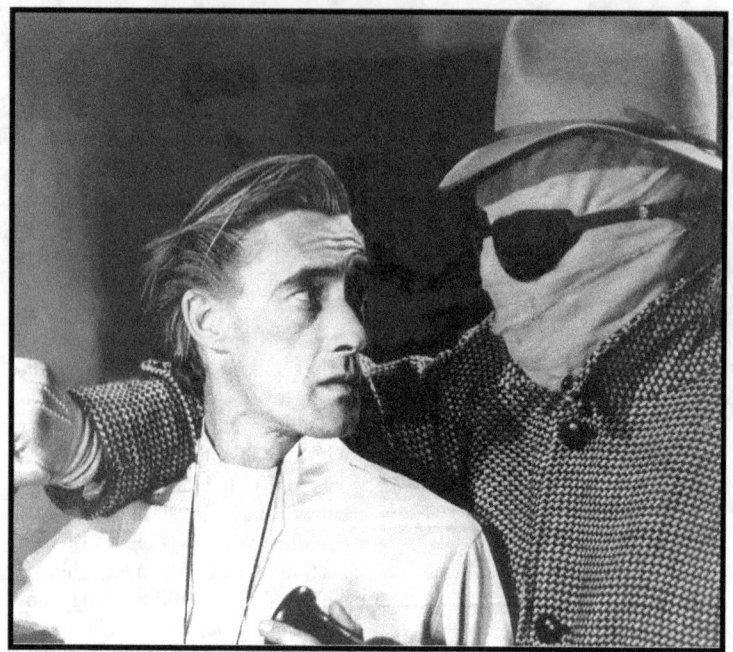

sequence shows the invisible man barely visible in the rain). This B production does impress in several sequences, though. One of the film's best sequences occurs when police spray a house with smoky gas to make the invisible man visible, yet cleverly, Geoffrey disguises himself as a policeman wearing a gas mask, so he seems like another cop in a household filled with policeman. Geoffrey approaches Helen (Nan Grey) and has her pretend to faint, so he can *rescue* her and take her outside to escape. Nice chills are generated here.

The film's best sequence is the eerie death of former night watchman Spears (Alan Napier), now superintendent (under Cobb, who will inherit the business from his brother Geoffrey and immediately ignores all the safety precautions his brother initiated). After Geoffrey toys with Spears' car, he announces his presence causing Spears to flee for his life in the woods, Geoffrey playfully laughing, pretending to be a ghost. Spears tells the truth, that Cobb was responsible for brother Michael's death. Geoffrey leaves Spears tied up in his mining home while he visits Cobb. In a wonderful sequence, Price holds a gun on Cobb, who is under protective custody, and forces him to leave the house. However, the cowardly fear Hardwicke creates with the enthusiastic vocal delivery of Price makes this a powerhouse sequence. Taking Cobb to the house where Spears is standing on a chair, a noose deliberately tied around his neck, Spears confesses that Cobb killed Michael, but foolishly, Geoffrey never realized how easy it would be for Cobb to kick the chair out from under Spears, thus hanging and instantly killing the only witness to the crime.

Overall, the film meanders without much horror or suspense, but in these few sequences the power of Vincent Price's vocal performance dominates (the sequence with Helen, Frank and Geoffrey having supper, Geoffrey dapper in dressing robe and bandages, becomes a high point with Geoffrey subtly revealing his disdain for feeble humanity and the hopes he has of becoming an all powerful ruler is a tribute to Vincent Price, the actor). *The Invisible Man Returns* is not even a great B production, but it does feature sequences of dramatic intensity that make it quite watchable.

The third direct sequel, *The Invisible Man's Revenge,* directed by Ford Beebe in 1944, features Jon Hall in his first starring role in Universal's invisibility entry. Taking a decidedly film noir nod, Hall, who escapes from a dockside ship, buys new clothing from an elderly haberdasher who asks too many questions, forcing the mysterious man, Robert Griffin, to get defensive and overbearing. Soon grabbing hold of his emotions, he politely exits but leaves behind a folded newspaper article showing him to be an escaped homicidal murderer with a blood trail in his recent past. Returning to visit

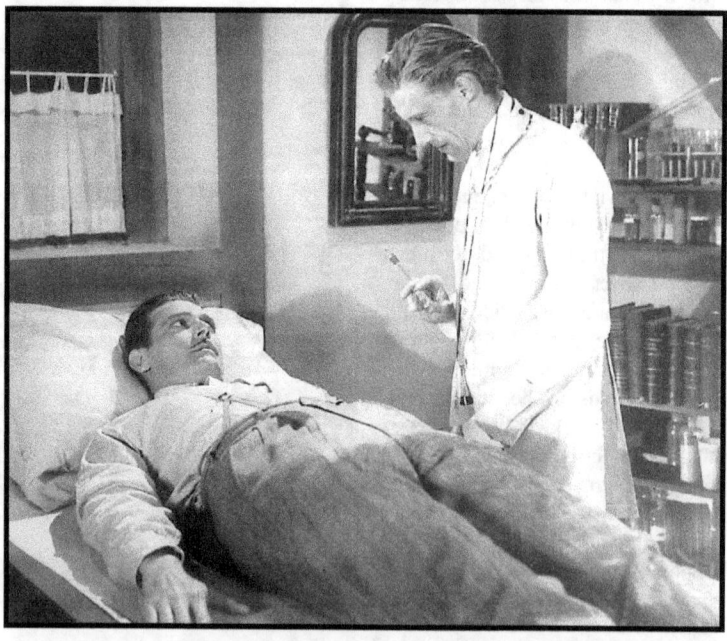

prim and proper Sir Jasper (Lester Matthews) and Lady Irene (Gale Sondergaard), the evil duo who left Griffin for dead in the jungle have benefited from finding a diamond mine, but the agreement was that all three parties should share equally, and Griffin wants his cut. The other two claim the fortune is gone, wasted on bad investments. Griffin is not satisfied when Jasper offers to give him half of his personal cash resources. Soon they drug him and have him thrown off the property, but they keep his copy of the financial arrangement and want him out of the way, forever.

Griffin becomes a fugitive and seeks shelter at the home of Dr. Drury (John Carradine) whose eyes light up: "fugitive… no friends!" Griffin realizes things are strange when he sees an invisible dog in a cage and a birdcage swing with an invisible parrot squawking away. Soon loud barking occurs from outside and an invisible dog on a leash enters. Griffin volunteers to become the doctor's guinea pig and be turned invisible, but after the experiment proves successful, Griffin pushes the old doctor aside and heads toward Jasper's house to claim his fortune. Forcing Jasper to sign a confession, Griffin is almost clunked over the head by devious Jasper but manages to elude the flying chair.

Soon Griffin finds himself falling in love with the beautiful Julie (Evelyn Ankers, in a bland role) and wants to get pretty boy Mark (Alan Curtis) out of her life, even if that means murder. Finding out a full body transfusion will turn him temporarily visible, Griffin drains the doctor of all his blood and sets his home afire, seeking refuge in Sir Jasper's home. Soon he is joined by Cockney comic relief Herbert Higgins (Leon Errol) who wants a cut of the good life, but Griffin offers him money to kill the loyal hound of the dead doctor who stalks the evil Griffin as far as Jasper's home, waiting outside howling and moaning.

The film's best moments occur near the end when Griffin, speaking to Julie and Mark, begins to turn invisible without warning. Cross-cutting shots of a transparent Jon Hall with actor Jon Hall wearing heavy pancake makeup, the panicky victim runs to his room covering his head with a sweater and seeks refuge in the bathroom, his entire head now invisible. This leads to Griffin's scheme to lure Mark down to the wine cellar. Griffin desires to kill Mark so Julie will now be his alone by draining Mark's body of blood to turn Griffin visible once again. The thrilling climax features the locked-in Mark reacting to the invisible one's taunts and throwing of objects, finally finding himself overwhelmed and knocked unconscious with a bottle of wine over his head. The invisible man almost manages to kill Mark as Griffin turns semi-visible, as the police break through the cellar door and a vicious dog attacks and kills Griffin. Once again, *The Invisible Man's Revenge* is perhaps a hair better than *The Invisible Man Returns*, even though the characters in *Revenge* are far less sympathetic. Both sequels are fine B productions, each offering 80-odd minutes of fun and excitement.

Surprisingly, Jon Hall played an undercover wartime spy two years earlier in 1942's *The Invisible Agent*, which is another pleasant entry in the invisible man series. The movie, caught up in World War II Nazi spy shenanigans, features Hall as the grandson of the original Invisible Man who keeps the formula hidden in his small print shop that is visited by five Nazi spies, including Stauffer (Cedric Hardwicke) and the Baron (Peter Lorre). Forcing Griffin to close his shop early, the band of criminals wants Griffin's invisibility formula to help their war effort, and they want it now. The Peter Lorre character notices a wonderful cutting blade on one piece of press equipment and forces Hall's hand underneath, slowly pressing down on the blade forcing the poor victim to talk. Giving in to pressure, Griffin screams to stop the torture, shouting he will get them the formula, which he produces from a hidden department in his desk drawer. However, in the ruckus the front store window is smashed, and Griffin is able, with a few well-placed punches and kicks, to escape with the formula. Soon making a deal with the U.S. government who want him to use the formula to turn one of their best agents invisible, Griffin insists he be made the guinea pig and carry out the mission.

In a wonderful special effects sequence, Griffin parachutes from the heavily bombarded plane, and as he slowly descends, he turns invisible with his harness and chute still descending to the ground. Griffin finally lands on a rooftop where he escapes. Soon he is romancing the elegant Nazi character portrayed by Ilona Massey, who is ultimately revealed to be an American agent. During the course of events, Griffin again meets up with Cedric Hardwicke and Peter Lorre who make quite effective villains. By the film's end Lorre commits hara-kiri with a knife and Griffin is rescued and returned to America, now with love interest Massey. But beforehand, the film features several marvelous special effects sequences, most impressively a sequence where Griffin dons a bathrobe and applies cream to his face and hands to be visible to Massey. Only the circles around his eyes remain invisible, but he dons dark glasses to finish the illusion. Unlike Jon Hall's character in *Revenge*, here in *The Invisible Agent* he is truly the pulp hero who is willing to sacrifice his life for the cause of freedom and the victory of the United States. It is a propaganda-filled B production, but it is one that approximates the thrills and chills of the world of serials and this movie could have inspired an entire invisibility espionage series all by itself.

Finally, the most comical entry here, 1940's *The Invisible Woman*, features a fading John Barrymore and Virginia Bruce as the title character. Perhaps this is the least successful movie in the series (interestingly enough, the screenplay was written by the team most responsible for writing some of the best Abbott and Costello movie scripts) and is played for comedy effect only. Even though the reliable John P. Fulton is once again employed for the invisibility effects, generally such gimmicks here underwhelm. Perky Virginia Bruce is just right as Kitty, but even her required nude sequence behind the screen fails to sizzle. John Barrymore, reduced to ham-fisted roles in less spectacular movie projects, is really quite good in this underplayed heavily made-up performance. He plays the whacky scientist whose projects are undermined by the son of a wealthy patron who has just gone broke from financial excess. Instead of being able to offer a volunteer $3,000 to be turned invisible, Professor Gibbs (Barrymore) can only offer the thrill but no compensation. But that's enough for Kitty, who wants to use her momentary invisibility to gain revenge on the nasty boss who fired her from her modeling job for speaking her mind.

The movie's minimal plot develops when a gangster bunch moves in on the professor, the gang including the comic Shemp Howard whose funniest scene involves him being knocked unconscious wearing a fish bowl over his head. Also the gifted comedian Charles Ruggles plays the flippant and wisecracking butler George, but the role as written does not allow Ruggles much of an opportunity to dazzle.

The movie, light on comedy, special effects and plot, ends with a newborn baby suddenly turning invisible. Perhaps the best performance in the movie belongs to the fading John Barrymore whose professor is warm, zany and comical when needed to be. However, when compared to the other movies, this A. Edward Sutherland–directed B production is bare bones at best. Not enough of a supporting role by Margaret Hamilton can save this non-entity.

When taken together, this Universal Legacy boxed-set offers preminium value for the dollar, as all these movies have been remastered to fine-grain perfection. The only extras, besides the documentary hosted by Rudy Behlmer and his audio commentary on the James Whale original, are a photo gallery and trailers. However the low list cost for this set makes it very attractive. Even if the Invisible Man series is mediocre at best, it is still a B series worth revisiting. And its success will allow others to come.

Ju-On
Movie: 3.5; Disc: 3.5
[Lions Gate DVD]

Just as the decades of the 1960s and 1970s creatively sparked by Italian horror cinema, the horror of the Millennium seems to belong to Asia (Japan and Korea), who are producing cutting-edge horror cinema. Americans might be talking about *The Grudge* (*Ju-On* was the original Japanese version) and *The Ring*, but the original Asian movies must be commended.

What makes Japanese horror movies so exciting is the fact that these movies return to what I've always labeled atmospheric horror, the type of shock sequence that punctuates a slow-building terror sequence based upon cinematography, editing and general creepiness, abetted by characters about whom we care. We can go back to the Val Lewton productions and his infamous "walks" and "buses" to get that atmospheric jolt, or more recently, Mario Bava's "A Drop of Water" sequence from *Black Sabbath* comes closest to becoming the thermometer for such eerily mounted chills. And in this modern era of special effects chills and splatter-heavy shock sequences, it is wonderful to be returning to an era where chills are no longer cheap and audiences are forced to look at the screen through clenched fingers over the eyes (as one of the leads in *Ju-On* does in the climax).

The structure of *Ju-On*, each separate sequence focusing on one character who is a victim of the ghostly haunted house, allows the house and its history of a wife and six-year-old child brutally murdered by an irate husband to remain front and center. Interestingly, as more and more characters are introduced, some overlap in the lives of others, and by the movie's end we see the bond between many of these characters that was not apparent while each individual sequence was presented. Thus, the piece-meal structure of the narrative is innovative and clever, but the use of sound, cinematography and acting congeal to produce one of the most exciting horror movies of the decade. And youthful director/writer Takashi Shimizu has a firm control of both interest and shock.

Like the little girl who dies in the well in *Ringu* and crawls outside the television screen, the ghost of *Ju-On* played by Takako Fuji is creepily haunting. She is shown crawling upward under bed covers toward her victim; she is shown bent and hovering over her victim who lies in bed; she comes upward between a victim whose hands cover her eyes; and most hauntingly, she crawls on her belly, snakelike, squirming, as though her backbone were broken, across the floor and down a staircase. And her easily identified calling card is her clicking, gurgling sound that announces her proximity to unaware victims. Her also dead son, portrayed by Ryota Koyama, is also strikingly haunting. Whether he, stone face, peers from behind the staircase grilling, dashes across the room behind adults or suddenly appears hunched in a closet or standing by the edge of a bed, his pancake makeup, dark eyes and icy stare proclaim that he is not among the living. His mother, strangely enough, sometimes appears as brown ectomorphic fog with darkly hidden eyes that is able to eerily envelop victims.

While *Ju-On* is more an exercise in short segmented horror where visuals and mood mean more than plot, ultimately, all the pieces of the puzzle do strangely come together at the end (the only exception is the appearance of the cat-ghost). Even when the narrative dangles momentarily, the haunting visuals and youthful actors simply reacting to mesmerizing horror is sublime. *Ju-On* becomes a creepy, unsettling and visual tour-de-force of horror, where acting, visuals and sound merge to create perhaps one of the most unsettling horror films of the decade. Movies such as *Ringu, Ju-On* and *The Eye* are creating the new lexicon of horror cinema, and isn't it about time something saved the limp horror film genre.

The Grudge
Movie: 3.0; Disc: 3.5
[Columbia/TriStar DVD]

Sam Raimi's Ghost House Pictures had the best intentions for remaking the Japanese *Ju-On* as *The Grudge,* an American language remake, using the same Japanese director Takashi Shimizu and his major crewmembers to rethink the movie for American audiences. *The Grudge* was even filmed in Japan with a mostly Japanese cast.

Fans can purchase *Ju-On* on DVD and chose to either see an English subtitled version or a sensitively dubbed version, but Raimi understands the bias that many horror movie fans here in the States hold toward foreign-produced movies. One thing is sure, people here have been exposed to *The Grudge* in ways they would never have been exposed to *Ju-On,* and this is a good thing.

I was very critical as I watched *The Grudge*, seeing vanilla Sarah Michelle Gellar and lover Jason Behr make Asian horror palpable for America, but her performance connected as the movie unrolled. For the most part, I was disappointed that the American version seemed to be almost a virtual remake of the Japanese original, until the final third of the movie. In that segment, American screenwriter Stephen Susco, working with Shimizu,

improved upon the plot of the original and explained the motive, the extramarital affair, that led to the murders and the haunting of the house. For keeping the best of the Japanese original, and for improving the story's final act, *The Grudge* deserves to be judged on its own.

I do believe the dark ectoplasmic ghost with haunting eyes is better in the American remake simply because the funds and improved special effects were available; however, some aspects work far better in the original. For instance, the subplot with the group of schoolgirls who visit their friend who lives isolated in her bedroom has been dropped in favor of creating the American Bill Pullman character. Also, the ghostly little boy is far more insidious and haunting in the original, and when the camera pans over to view him staring from atop the stairs in the original, audiences jump; here in the American remake, we hardly bat an eyelid. The Japanese policeman in the Japanese original is more sympathetic and more richly drawn than his Asian counterpart in the American remake. The unsettling, almost comatose mother in the Japanese original is much more unworldly and creepy than Grace Zabriski, in the remake. Overall, the original Japanese horror sequences seem to have the edge over the U.S. counterparts (the frightened ghost who balloons up under the covers, her terrifying face emerging from the edge of the covers, terrifies the viewer more effectively in the original than in the remake). However, Geller's American-in-Japan character that seems to have a difficult time adjusting to an alien culture adds an air of malaise that was missing in the all-Asian-cast original. Ultimately, both films have been created by the same vision and directorial eye, and while over half of both films are nearly identical, the differences are significant. Both films shine in their ability to terrify in new inventive visual ways.

The Grudge contains a five-part documentary involving on-the-set production details and interviews with the cast and crew. A documentary on fear is also interesting. An audio commentary is included.

One thing is certain, Americans should look to Asia (not only Japan but Korea as well) to find the best in horror cinema today, and while Americans still focus on nonstop action and special makeup effects, Asia has returned to the more difficult arena of atmospheric chills that resonate by getting under the skin. Hopefully America will learn to do this on its own and not feel compelled to remake every superior Asian horror movie imported to our shores. That will get old fast.

Ed Wood
Movie: 3.5; Disc: 3.5
[Touchstone DVD]

For me, this is director Tim Burton's finest cinematic moment and it is among only a handful of movies directed toward the classic and low-budget horror movie audience. I raved about the movie upon its initial release, and the film continues to dazzle with its spot on set design, inspired casting and brilliant performance by Johnny Depp. True, Bela Lugosi supposedly never cursed in actual life and Ed Wood was probably much seedier and alcoholic than Burton's vision allows, but this is not the standard bio film.

The central theme of the movie is launched loud and clear when Ed Wood and Dolores Fuller are in bed discussing their future plans together, and Wood, in low-rent desperation, questions if he has what it takes to be an artist. And that's what this movie is about... ordinary people living their lives in quiet desperation, Ed Wood breaking on through by shear virtue of his non-ending optimism reinforced by his carny/showman trickery. I see it all the time in my business... students who believe they have what it takes to become surgeons... when they don't; writers who think they have a professional style to get published and sell... when they don't; amateur filmmakers who feel they have produced the best movie since *Citizen Kane*... when they come up far short. So many people delude themselves to think they are talented when they are not, at least not yet. This is what *Ed Wood* is about... not accepting the no talent stance directed by other people, fortifying the delusion of talent, acting upon that delusion and producing a personal work of art that shines despite its limitations (as idol Orson Welles advises Wood in one of the film's highlight sequences: don't waste your life making someone else's vision come true). And as the house lights go down on the premiere of *Plan 9 From Outer Space*, the effervescent Wood proclaims, "This is the one they'll remember me for," and in his delusion, he was 100% correct. Even working with a very low budget, compromising some of his artistic vision to just make the movie (casting a no talent in the lead of *Bride of the Monster*, insisted on by the investor) and looking at the big picture (ignoring the fact that most of his sets looked cheap and unrealistic), Ed Wood managed to create idiosyncratic movies that were unlike any other movies ever produced, and for remaining true to such a vision, Wood, in spite of or because of his lack of talent, became a Hollywood visionary, a man who loved his work and always tried to do the best he could. Honestly admitting to living his life with a nonjudgmental nature and always encouraging his cast and crew, Wood admits he would never have any friends otherwise. And this was his true strength as an artist... Wood chose what to ignore, what was unimportant, and he never allowed anyone to convince him otherwise. Perhaps he looked at the world through rose-colored glasses, but this distorted vision became the only artistic vision for Wood.

With Howard Shore's wonderful musical score, using *Swan Lake* as Lugosi's motif; the quirky ensemble acting including a wonderful performance from George "The Animal" Steele, the Academy Award-winning performance of Bela Lugosi by Martin Landau and Johnny Depp's essential performance that carries the entire movie on his shoulders; the wonderful black and white photography of Stefan Czapsky; and the wildly amusing (if not always historically accurate) script, *Ed Wood* becomes a movie that captures perfectly the low-budget mentality of the underbelly of Hollywood filmmaking. But it also captures a drug-addicted 74-year-old Lugosi fortifying himself with whiskey before preparing to dive into a small lake to wrestle with a motorless mechanical octopus at 4 a.m., and making the performance shine. Ed Wood, to the best of his ability, rewards his idol Lugosi by writing a particularly moving speech for him at the climax of the movie, and Lugosi is grateful for all the opportunities accorded him at this, the lowest ebb of his career, where a little of the old magic is allowed to radiate a while longer.

Ultimately, *Ed Wood*, though it contains doses of humor, is ultimately a heart-felt and emotional drama that touches the hearts of all of us who celebrate such seat-of-the-pants filmmaking. The audience comes to accept Ed Wood's delusions and celebrate his determination to create art against all odds. Every one of us who always wanted to sing, but couldn't, wanted to dance, but couldn't, wanted to do that one thing, but couldn't, will shed a tear at Ed Wood's tri-umphs, the ordinary man who faced impossible odds with such optimism and determination.

The extras contained on this long-delayed DVD release feature multiple documentaries filmed during production with interviews with cast and crew, an audio commentary track, a documentary on the Theremin, a sexy and haunting music video that is true to the spirit of the movie and a pristine 16:9 enhanced widescreen print. For me, *Ed Wood* just gets better and better with age, for its message speaks loudly to the ordinary people who look to the stars and beyond.

Shaun of the Dead
Movie: 3.5; Disc: 3.5
[Universal DVD]

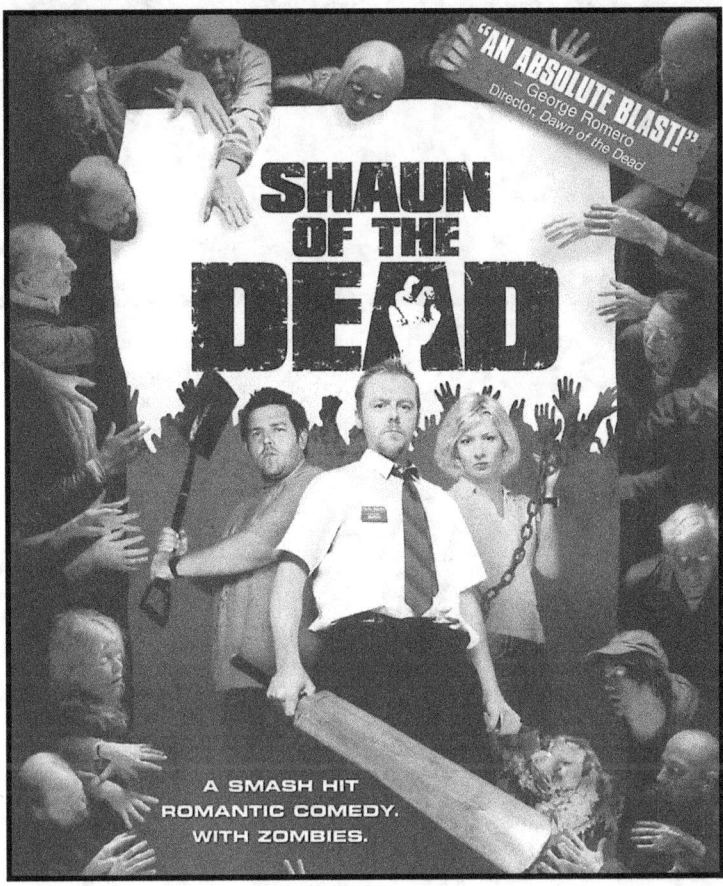

Who would think that in the wake of the zombie revival of late that *Shaun of the Dead*, a marvelous little British anomaly, would become a significant movie release? Director Edgar Wright and his co-writer Simon Pegg (also who stars as Shaun) do everything right: They cleverly reference the past ("We're coming for you, Barbara"; the zombies move slowly; visual silhouettes of hands and arms outside the Winchester bar remind audiences of Romero-style visuals); they offer rich movie characters created by able professionals; they make humorous social commentary (the credit sequence); and the movie is original enough that it does not merely retrace the same steps of the past. In fact, the major way this film distinguishes itself from a rash of others is by its cleverness and intelligence. The way the camera pans over today's culture of zombies—zombified supermarket clerks serving lines of zombied customers, as we pan outside and see youth zombified by their iPods as we finally pan to the bare legs and feet of Shaun who stumbles, zombie-like, into his living room awakening from a night's sleep, yawning and making zombie sounds. Such a brilliant sequence is only one of many such sequences. Other clever sequences involve Shaun and Ed (Nick Frost) going through their case of vinyl records deciding which ones to sacrifice to defeat the onslaught of two zombies (ultimately deciding on girlfriend's Sade album). Finally, the visual differentiation between Shaun's first morning jaunt to the local convenience shop and the second day is simply marvelous. Day one Shaun dodges two cars as he crosses the street, he passes plenty of people alive and active, he sees a black man wash his car and the store is clean and has plenty of newspapers on the counter. His walk home with his snacks is noneventful. Day two the streets are deserted, overturned trashcans liter the neighborhood, the formerly washed car has its windshield smashed in, the convenience store has bloody hand prints on glass doors and Shaun, in classic slapstick slide, almost falls on the bloody floor and after exiting the store leaving change (no cashier is to be seen and no newspapers on the counter) for his stuff, Shaun confronts a panhandler who asked him for money yesterday, who is now a zombie, and the panhandler acts exactly the same. Again Shaun is oblivious to his surroundings: On his walk home he ignores zombies and dead bodies littered all over the neighborhood.

At its heart *Shaun of the Dead* is a relationship story between Shaun and his girlfriend of two years, Liz (Kate Ashfield), who wants more of a commitment out of Shaun, who basically is a slacker who seems far more compatible with his child-man roommate and boyhood friend Ed. As third roommate screams at Shaun, "You better sort your... life out!" And with his dead-end electronic sales job and strained relationship with his step-dad (the wonderful Bill Nighly), we can see how utterly zombified Shaun's life has become. Only when he slowly comes to accept that his own life is turning against him and he sees the need to fight for a real, actual existence, does Shaun emerge as the slacker hero who saves his girlfriend, even if the bodies of others are left by the wayside.

Shaun of the Dead becomes the most original and ultimately satisfying zombie film of its era (the remake of *Dawn of the Dead*, more visceral, comes close) and once again demonstrates that effective horror movies can be produced in the new millennium. Extras abound including outtakes, extended on-air TV shows, documentaries and interviews with cast and crew, Simon Pegg's video diary, audition tapes, etc. *Shaun of the Dead* bears up well under repeat viewings and the film reveals such charms under such scrutiny.

BOOK REVIEWS

Smirk, Sneer and Scream: Great Acting in Horror Cinema by Mark Clark (McFarland); $43.95 postpaid (order 800-253-2187)

Midnight Marquee staffer Mark Clark's first book is a beauty, one that examines the often overlooked contribution of film acting to the horror cinema, both past and present. While I may have preferred a book devoted solely to the earlier decades of classic horror, the book is balanced between the old and new. And such a balance creates a richer, even more insightful retrospective examining the contributions of both horror film icons and mainstream actors to horror film history.

Part One details the horror stars including Lon Chaney, Boris Karloff, Bela Lugosi, Lionel Atwill, Dwight Frye, Peter Lorre, John Carradine, George Zucco, Lon Chaney, Jr., Vincent Price, Peter Cushing, Christopher Lee and others.

Part Two details mainstream actors who occasionally created horror performances, actors such as Fredric March, Charles Laughton, Anthony Perkins, Michael Rooker, Anthony Hopkins, Haley Joel Osment and many others.

Examining a sample entry—Boris Karloff—his chapter begins with a two-page bio that covers all the bases. Then several iconic films are specifically covered, both the movies themselves and Karloff's performance. In the Karloff chapter the author examines *Frankenstein, The Mummy, The Black Cat, The Black Room, The Walking Dead, The Body Snatcher, Targets* and a section on "Other Notable Performances." Unfortunately, what many consider Karloff's greatest performance, his Monster from *Bride of Frankenstein*, only warrants a few paragraphs as part of the 1931 *Frankenstein* coverage, along with his lesser performance from *Son of Frankenstein*. However, author Clark has every right to consider Karloff's initial performance as the Monster to be the defining one for all three 1930s Frankenstein movies. And Clark does pay the icon his dues.

What entertained and challenged me the most about Clark's intelligent book was that I found myself speaking back to him, as I read page after page, often in harsh, angry terms, but at other times, commending Clark about his perceptions and intelligence. That's what is so fascinating about critiquing an actor's performance... so many different opinions and so many different ways to reflect.

Mark Clark's book comes heavily recommended for its insight, breezy style and balance between the old and new. *Smirk, Sneer and Scream* is a book that may state more than a few controversial opinions, but such opinions are always explained, supported and peppered with humor and a total lack of pretense. Dare I say the book is a fun read?!!!

Review by Gary J. Svehla

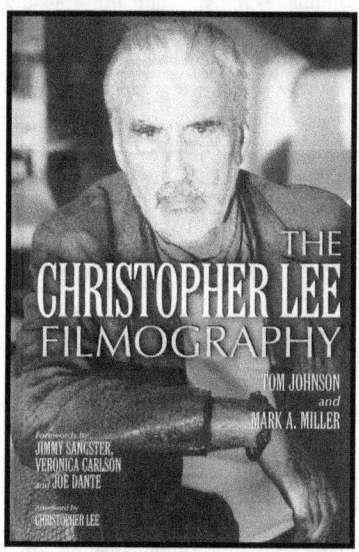

The Christopher Lee Filmography by Tom Johnson and Mark A. Miller (McFarland); $59.00 postpaid (order 800-253-2187)

With forewords by Jimmy Sangster, Veronica Carlson and Joe Dante, and an afterword by Christopher Lee, this five-year-in-the-making filmography covers all of Lee's films released from 1948 to 2003. This massive 460-page book is essential reading for all fans of Christopher Lee.

Authors Tom Johnson and Mark A. Miller, both MidMar staffers, do a masterful job of covering each film, their critiques augmented with personal reflections from Christopher Lee. Each entry is divided into credits, cast, synopsis, commentary and remembrances from Lee. The two-page coverage given *City of the Dead* (*Horror Hotel* in the U.S.) contains the commentary: "Lee embellishes his role with remarkable, subtle facial movements that reveal his inner fear of discovery. In the case of Driscoll, however, Lee slips in a self-satisfied arrogant type of evil that reveals itself in glimpses as he manipulates other characters to their doom." Such a style is easily understood yet insightful coming from two critical minds that know their subject matter backwards and forwards. The point I stress here is that by reading this book one is not merely getting rehash or the same critical points made in other books that examine the film career of Christopher Lee. Johnson and Miller offer fresh, intelligent insight. And Christopher Lee, in his own commentary, offers: "This was a Lovecraft-like story, very different from the other Gothic films I'd been doing at the time... This film had great atmosphere, was wonderfully photographed... This is a good time that has held up well. I believe it's more popular now than ever, especially in America, possibly because of the American New England setting." While Lee's reflections are always interesting, his own understanding of what exactly makes his films work is not always as perceptive as the comments of Johnson and Miller. Ask any American horror fan why *City of the Dead* is a great horror film, and I do not think even one would say because of the foggy, stage-bound English sets that try to duplicate New England by way of American International. But what we have are the two extremes. First we have the movie critics who dissect the virtue of every production and specifically focus on Lee's contribution as actor. Second, we have the actor himself reflect upon his own feelings of making the movie or vividly state the lasting impressions the film made after the fact. Together, such a teaming is thoroughly intelligent and entertaining, all at the same time.

Several appendices are also included, including short films, television series appearances and miniseries. However, this is the type of book one doesn't necessarily read from first page to last, but it's a chronological listing of all Christopher Lee's feature films, so fans can check out coverage of their favorite Hammer film or go straight to the end with *Lord of the Rings*. Such a wonderful legacy to the enduring career of Christopher Lee, *The Christopher Lee Filmography* by Tom Johnson and Mark A. Miller clearly demonstrates the authors' lifetime of dedication to this final horror film icon still working in 2005.

Review by Gary J. Svehla

Ray Harryhausen—An Animated Life by Ray Harryhausen, Billboard/Watson-Guptill, 2004. Hardcover, dust jacket, illustrated, 303 pages, $50.00.

An Animated Life by Ray Harryhausen (with Tony Dalton) is a major book for fans and students of stop-motion animation. Since the early 1950s, Harryhausen has thrilled audiences on the big screen with creatures such as tyrannosaurus, cyclops, fighting skeletons, giant crabs, aliens, mammoths, giant octopuses, flying harpies, seven-headed hydra and a flying winged horse.

The author put out his first book Film Fantasy Scrapbook over 30 years ago, and then he was reluctant about revealing his illusion tricks. In this new attractively designed book, the author seems driven to leave no illusion cloaked in mystery. Though the text has been expanded considerably, this edition is backed up with an equal amount of illustrations and never-seen photos and storyboards. Though other books exist on stop-motion animation, this book casts a shadow over all its predecessors. Here, Harryhausen finally reveals the inner workings behind the process combining actors and animated models on the big screen, which he originally called Dynamation.

Harryhausen traces his fascination with film fantasy on the big screen to its earliest beginnings when he first saw *The Lost World* and *King Kong*. Deservedly, he credits his parents for encouraging his interest, especially his father who constructed many of the metal armatures for his creations. He tells of first meeting his mentor Willis O'Brien, the artist who gave him some valuable constructive criticism which the young animator never forgot.

After getting his first professional experience as an animator working for George Pal's *Puppetoons* and landing an apprentice animator's job on the big-budgeted *Mighty Joe Young*, he eventually won the job of being in charge of all the animation on *The Beast from 20,000 Fathoms* (a film, Harryhausen reveals, whose animation budget was so low he had to make up the difference out of his own pocket!). It was not until Harryhausen worked on *It Came from Beneath the Sea* that he met producer Charles H. Schneer who shared his dreams and became producer and collaborator on nearly every one of Harryhausen's movies.

Following two ventures into science fiction, Harryhausen made *The 7th Voyage of Sinbad*, the first of his legendary mythological fantasies. It was also his first film in color and color created new challenges for his Dynamation process.

The author gives a sympathetic portrait of his idol Willis O'Brien, whom Harryhausen described as a pioneer and innovator in the business, but O'Brien, according to Harryhausen, lacked the necessary drive to put his ideas across to the Hollywood producers. Instead, O'Brien was ignored by the industry and was simply considered a technician.

An additional plus at the end of the book is a treat for Harryhausen fans... a chapter on unrealized projects such as *The Abominable Snowman, Adventures of Baron Munchausen, Tarzan and the Ant Men, War Eagles* and *Fall of the House of Usher*. The only drawback in this book is a lack of an index.

Review by "Bojak"

GRAVE DIGGINGS

Dear Gary and Susan:

An episode occurred during a theatrical showing of *Devil Girl from Mars* that I never saw mentioned in any of many discussions of the film both in print and over the Internet.

Here is the article published in the Charleston, SC *News & Courier*, July 13, 1956, Page 5-B:

HIS CLOTHES AFLAME, BOY DISTURBS MOVIE

Akron, Ohio, July 12 (AP)—A movie audience was watching The *Devil Girl from Mars* in the Strand Theater yesterday when a screaming youth, his pants in flames, ran into the room and started rolling on the floor.

A man grabbed the boy, ripped off his shirt and used it to smother the fire.

The boy, Daniel Hallinan, 14, son of Councilman Joseph T. Hallinan of nearby Barberton, blamed the blaze on a leaking can of lighter fluid.

He said he had been sitting in the theater when he felt his pants getting damp. He went to a restroom to discover the cause and said he lit a cigarette lighter before he realized the can of lighter fluid in his pocket was leaking.

Imagine the potential for publicity for the movie. "*Devil Girl from Mars*... so hot and sexy, she set a young man's pants on fire!" The above incident seems to be virtually forgotten today, except by myself, but by sending it out to film fans, I'm hoping it might give some fresh angle to reviewing a film that has probably been reviewed enough already.

Fred Hamilton

Dear Gary and Susan:

First of all, the Universal Legacy Collection (*Frankenstein, Dracula, The Wolf Man, The Mummy, Creature from the Black Lagoon, The Invisible Man*, etc.) is beyond excellent—fabulous picture and sound and fans just must love all the extras, especially the commentaries. I was slightly apprehensive when I saw that Tom Weaver was doing the audio commentary for *The Wolf Man* and was quite pleased that for once he didn't bring up Lon Chaney's drinking problems. Weaver is great at what he does, but he always seems to dwell on that sad subject.

Other recent spectacular releases include *The Old Dark House, The Ghoul, Freaks, Dawn of the Dead* four pack, The Lon Chaney Collection and the *Dr. Jekyll and Mr. Hyde* double feature with superb commentary by Greg Mank.

I even broke down and bought the *Dark Shadows* DVD series. I thought it was the greatest when I was younger (and yes, like most baby boomers my age, 43, I did run home from school to watch it on TV). Although the series does contain its share of tedium, many episodes contain quality acting and well-generated scares, all despite the particularly low budget the afternoon series was allotted.

"So good they're bad"… is that the truth? I have a soft sci-fi spot for all those "B" movies that at least tried, despite the lack of funds, equipment, thespian talent, etc. Indeed, I enjoy most of them more than the tedious, over-budgeted junk that has come out the past several years (*The Wild, Wild West, James and the Giant Peach, Armageddon, Scream* and its sequels, just to name a few). I will always enjoy such off-the-wall fare as *The Manster, I Was a Teenage Frankenstein, The Killer Shrews, The Flesh Eaters, The Severed Arm* (a 1973 offering with Deborah Walley and Motel 6 interiors that has a certain kinetic charm to it), *The Tingler* and almost any late 1950s/early 1960s Mexican horror films released to American TV by K. Gordon Murray.

I loved the recent Mad Doctor retrospective in MidMar. Almost all of those mad medics have a special place on my movie shelf, especially George Zucco, Ernest Thesiger, Vincent Price, Colin Clive and Peter Cushing. There are several performances that did not make the list and deserve to have some notice:

John Carradine in *The Unearthly* (1957). Carradine just absolutely, positively and with pure panache

chews the scenery as only he could. Lines to relish include: "There, my dear fellow, is your problem!" or "You told me a fabricated story that wouldn't fool a child," or "Wipe my brow."

Basil Rathbone in *The Black Sleep* (1956). His Dr. Cadman is quietly ruthless as he tries to bring his dead wife back to life.

Claudio Brook in *Samson in the Wax Museum* (1963). Those K. Gordon Murray Mexican movies are like a big bowl of fudge from The Candy Kitchen. They may be junky, but they are so good you just cannot resist. From a quiet low-key performance in the first half hour, Brook's Dr. Karol descends into extreme heavy-handed ham fests, giving such stars as Bela Lugosi, Vincent Price and Basil Rathbone a good run for their money.

Steve Schimming

Hello Gary:

Today I found your excellent magazine *Midnight Marquee* in Tower Books. I was amazed at all of the great information in this one publication. I enjoyed the mad doctors feature and I must admit I highly enjoyed Boris Karloff's performance as Dr. Niemann in *House of Frankenstein* and Jeffrey Combs' title role in *Re-Animator*. The only disagreement I had was I enjoyed Marlon Brando in the role of Dr. Moreau more than Charles Laughton. Brando was a very seasoned actor and he made

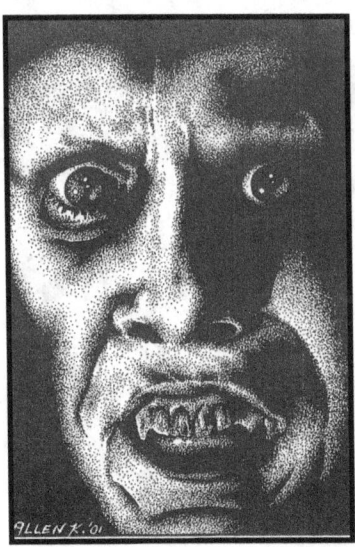

Moreau seem so real, but he also made his character in *Apocalypse Now* seem real. There is something about Marlon Brando that can give you the creeps.

Paul Dale Roberts

Dear Gary:

Thanks very much for the new issue of *Midnight Marquee*. The plethora of still photographs was worth the price of admission by itself. Your reviews were also especially interesting this time around. They have induced me to acquire the Legacy Universal *Dracula* box set to kick-start a more earnest transition to DVDs, so I'll finally be seeing the Spanish-language *Dracula* for the first time (hailed by many for its superior cinematography) along with David Skal's masterful documentary. Since I invariably begin delving into each issue with your reviews, I want to thank you for your attention to detail and thoughtful criticism in that department. When dealing with the release of such familiar films, reviews could easily become the intellectual equivalent of a dog chasing its own tail, as I have seen occur more than once in another genre publication. I agree wholeheartedly with your assessment of *House of Dracula*, even without seeing it yet on DVD. However, you were a bit harsh in comparing it to *House of Frankenstein*, which has marvelous visual sequences that make up for the segmented structure you mentioned.

I too prefer Onslow Stevens to Boris Karloff as best mad doctors pick in the Monster Rally House series, but other than that I agree totally with Lon Talbot's picks that lead off that frenetic survey. As for the worst horror films, I was surprised no one nominated either *Cry of the Bewitched or Valley of the Zombies*, two epics that I doubt anyone (even Mark Clark and Bryan Senn) could endure screening back-to-back. *From Hell it Came* is indeed a plodding invitation to drowsiness but let no one impugn the integrity of Paul Blaisdell's Tabonga!

Although James J.J. Janis' "She Has Always Lived in the Castle" is on the whole a fine article, I must take issue with his exaggerated claim that Anne Radcliffe's Gothic novels inspired "almost all of the Victorians from Dickens to Stoker and from Conan Doyle to Stevenson right into the 20th century and beyond." A more blatant attempt to shoehorn inaccurate

generalizations into one's thesis could hardly be imagined. When I read *The Mysteries of Udolpho*, somewhere in those timeworn pages of my past, my impression was that her innovations were entirely those pertaining to the suspense-building technique Janis noted. Her themes and settings are essentially clever treatments of existing literary archetypes and not something new. She was most certainly not an influence on Poe, except by some obscure process of osmosis known only to Mr. Janis. And of course Victorian literature is a bottomless pit in quantitative terms, so such statements as the one I quoted simply won't do, as Sherlock Homes might have said.

Among the many good illustrations for the essay, that of the beautiful, unequalled Fay Wray was poignant because I received the issue on the very day her passing was announced on the network news. I look forward to reading tributes to her storied career in the next issues of *Filmfax* and *Scarlet Street*, and hope one of your talented house writers will do an in depth feature on her work that will cover not only classics like *The Most Dangerous Game* and *Mystery of the Wax Museum*, but seldom-seen films such as *Woman in the Shadows* and others.

John Hitz

Dear Mr. Svehla:

How about an issue devoted to those timeless heroes of Sword and Sandal epics? Quite a few such films bordered on fantasy, science fiction and horror.

Steve Reeves, Gordon Scott, Reg Park, Mark Forrest, Ed Fury, Alan Steel, Kirk Morris, Dan Vadis, Rock Madison... all classic screen musclemen worth featuring. Even Rory Calhoun did one, *The Colossus of Rhodes*, without his Stetson hat or six guns anywhere in sight.

These movies have strong fan bases and are lovingly remembered. Some titles include *Hercules in the Haunted World, Goliath and the Dragon, Samson and the Seven Miracles of the World, Son of Hercules in the Land of Fire, Goliath and the Vampires*, etc.

I had just as much fun watching these films as I did watching the horror and science fiction movies. It's time to remove the camp stigma placed on these films and give them their rightful place in film history. It's time this genre receives the respect it so rightfully deserves. Remember, each genre has a following all its own.

I've seen noses turned up, eyebrows raised with a sniff of snobby dismissal by hardcore horror movie lovers, some of whom consider Sword and Sandal epics beyond contempt, not worthy to be considered alongside even the B horror productions.

These films and their mighty heroes have a warm spot in this old kid's heart. Let all the people who dismiss such entertainment accept the fact that perhaps they wouldn't know a good time at the movies, even if it bit them.

Bill Wilkerson

www.ingramcontent.com/pod-product-compliance
Lightning Source LLC
Chambersburg PA
CBHW081728100526
44591CB00016B/2540